# Hitchhiking with Drunken Nuns

*A trip into open-hearted faith,
mystery, connection and creativity*

*To my Sons,*
*May the universe perform a miracle and grant you*
*all of this beauty with less of this pain.*

Hitchhiking with Drunken Nuns
Published by Proost Copyright 2019

All poems and images by Emily Garcés

www.proost.co.uk

# Acknowledgements

*If I have learnt anything it is that a life
without gratitude is dead on the inside.*

**The light that will never go out** – meeting you realigned me with the universe; losing you broke me into as many pieces as the stars. **Oliver and Tahiel** – you are the best children a mother could ask for. Your patience and kindness during this long period of writing has made the whole thing possible. Nothing I do could make me prouder than I am to be your mother. **Toria** – a friend who accompanies you into a place of such extreme darkness becomes more than a friend and more than a sister. You mean more to me than I mean to myself. I do not know where I stop and where you begin. **Andrea** – we got this. I feel like you are in possession of more of the contents of my head than I am. Have we shared so much that we have expanded into each other? I love you so much it hurts. **The Order of the Black Sheep** – what would I do without you – you wonderful bunch of weirdos. So much good food, so many good conversations. Thank you for putting the co-mutiny back into church. I thought I was the only one until I met you. **My Neighbours** – you make my house feel like a home within a home. Thank you so very much for putting up with me. **Rachel** – learning to write would have been a very different journey without you. **Mum** – your love of people and of animals and of colour changed how I see the world. **Dad** – you taught me that questions are worth more than answers and that curiosity is worth more than knowledge. **Chris and Andrew** – thank you for the holidays and for the house. You mean more to me than I can express. **Gran** – you taught me to paint and showed me that learning does not stop at childhood. I saw the world expanding inside you until you became bigger and more eternal than all those things you learned. **Tom** – thank you for the apple. **Quel** – thank you for letting me read your diaries for the chapter about our Christmas in the Andes. I think our brains share some of the same wiring. Not sure if you realise how much your presence in my life has stopped me from going insane. **Peter Rollins and the Pyrotheology community** – I had a Christian toothache all my life and tried all sorts of fillings and procedures. You gave me the bravery I needed to get the tooth pulled and to be proud of my gap-toothed smile. **Mike, Michael, Corey and The Liturgists community** – so cathartic, all of this talk, but you brought it all back to remembering how to love each other and opened a brave space for us all to heal. **Margaret, Joan and all the beautiful others I met online during those darkest of months** – you are angels. To feel your eyes watching from afar has been more of a comfort than you will ever know. **Getting Naked with Drunken Nuns** – this Facebook group full of beautiful people has shown me that it is possible to have vastly different backgrounds and opinions and to allow your own beliefs to become less monochrome as a result. **My Patreon Supporters** – I love you all. Thank you for your patience with me while so much of my head was in this book. **Andy and Anna Raine** – your presence in my world these past years has turned the air into something I want to inhale. Like two large trees breathing out huge amounts of oxygen into the ecosystem. You teach us smaller trees to stand tall and keep doing the same. **My Workawayers** – you know I would not have found the time to write this without you. It has become your book too because of that. There is not space here to mention you all by name, but there is space in my heart for all of you (sorry, but sometimes the truth is a little cheesy). **Merle** – what you did for my family was beyond the call of duty, danke schoen; I do not deserve you. **Indigo** – we do not need drugs; we are the drugs. **Paul** – you came into my world at all the right moments and taught me to taste the hell out of whatever life presents me with, without wrinkling my nose at any of it. **Andy and Margo** – you put the *rock* back in rock and roll. Your belief in me has been solid at a time when my survival depended on it. **Chrissie** – my life has been full of born-again experiences, my divorce was one of them, meeting you was another. Your very existence symbolises the beginning of something new for humanity. You saw my pain and held it in a way that no one else ever could. **Louise Warner** – my stranger on a train. That conversation with you was enough to help me let go and let trauma roll through my body like a guest and not a resident. I will never underestimate the value of talking to strangers. **Rev Bingo** – Your proof-reading skills earned you friend-for-life status. I owe you a gallon of good whisky. **Tess Hall** – You popped up from the rhizome with your ideas at just the right time. Do you think that was coincidence?

I am pretty sure that I do not have all the necessary qualifications needed to write a book – but I am hoping my array of skills and experiences will give me at least a small chance of success:

I am so tall, that a woman once exclaimed: *You are every child's dream!* when I reached the high branch of a tree to shake down hundreds of horse chestnuts. Using only a kayak, an IKEA bag, and a child's fishing net, I have rescued the swans on a nearby lake no less than five times – and was unfazed by their complete lack of gratitude. Without desiring to, I once peed publicly three times in the same day – and have yet to develop a fear of outdoor urination. I pushed two large babies out of my body without requiring pain relief or a hospital. I have been charged by a wild tapir.

At least four songs have been written about me: one from a mental ward, one as a jingle for my painting show, one to commemorate my midnight busking sessions in dark city centres, and one by a man who proposed five minutes after we met.

I am so connected to the divine, that a squirrel once fell on my head when I told God that I wanted to feel closer to nature. At the age of nineteen I engaged in an hour-long battle with a demonised cat in Argentina. I once prayed so hard that my body did not stop shaking for two weeks. Late one evening I figured out the meaning of life – but had forgotten it by morning. I can speak in tongues.

I have cycled across the United Kingdom on a whim. Taken eight hours to ride a broken bicycle up a mountain in Chile – and twenty minutes to ride down it. I have been known to ride a bike across Amsterdam whilst sitting on an armchair. I can mend a bicycle using nothing but shoelaces. I have inbuilt satellite navigation.

I swam across the eye of a volcano with an indigenous school child, who I kidnapped by accident. My clothes once exploded violently in front of a church youth group when I dived off a bridge in Bolivia. I have been known to skinny-dip in the dark guided and clothed by nothing but glowstick earrings. There is video footage of me walking by a lake at night to confront a T-Rex. I invented wild swimming.

I am currently surviving on foraged wild garlic. I once stung my tongue on undercooked nettles – and did not stop chewing. I regularly fed forty people in a warehouse in Buenos Aires, in a kitchen so small and so crowded that you could not bring your arms down if you entered whilst carrying a pan on your head. I insist on making my own bread whilst wild camping. When I am bored, I use powdered beetroot to make all my meals pink. I can eat everything but olives.

I was given a four-star rating by the Scotsman Newspaper for my John Cleese inspired acting abilities. I read all the Russian Authors as a child. I learnt Spanish by reading Anna Karenina. I can make my eyes look in different directions and inhale my top lip into my nostrils. I have been seen tidying up children's toys with my feet whilst carrying a baby and folding laundry. I can translate simultaneously and at high speed from Spanish to English whilst wondering if love travels like water in the weather system. I have ridden bareback in the wilds of Patagonia to round up cattle with gauchos who hang horse's heads on hooks in sheds. I have been sighted sliding gracefully down a Chilean glacier slowed only by a stone age hand tool. I can pluck a pheasant, orchestrate the creation of masterpieces by artistic novices, hold long conversations with Tawney Owls, and make the perfect cup of tea.

So, I am hoping that I will be able to write a book – though who knows what sort of a book it will be…

Writing about yourself is a very odd thing to do. Half of my perceptions are probably false. This book does not claim to be true, but it does document events according to how I remember them. I have never seen myself. I have looked in a mirror. I have seen photos. I walk around in this body like I am driving a car. I think I know what colour the car is, but I am just guessing. Seems a shame to limit you to this perspective, so I have asked a few friends to introduce me:

*I first met Emily Garces in the toilet of Chesterfield Labour club in 2015. She was like a Great Dane puppy, effervescent with love and bounce and giddiness, a whirlwind of womance and enthusiasm, wisdom and innocence. We delighted in our matching black hair and leather jackets. We had other things in common too, not least a zest for life which I had lost but knew was still in there somewhere and which Emily had a knack for reigniting in me. She instantly became the ying to my yang. She had an Enid Blyton childhood and I, well, had not, and it felt like the universe had brought us to one another to understand each other's worlds and fill in the missing bits.*

*She is without doubt the funniest person I know. She has an ability to make me laugh from deep down in my belly in a way that no one else can. There's a feistiness and fierce joyfulness about her that makes you realise you have not been living life quite enough. Emily sees the world through LSD eyes. She is all at once astonished and amused and fascinated by the smallest details and can find adventure and beauty in any situation. Whether that's a trip to B&Q or a model village, Emily makes you feel like you are playing the lead role in a Hollywood film. She will make you wear a yellow headscarf and shades and emits a vibe of celebrity which attracts special treatment wherever she goes. When I'm with Emily I feel like the child I always wanted to be, free and daft and mischievous. She makes me feel it is never too late to have a happy childhood.*

*Emily introduced me to colour. She told me if I wore bright things it would make me feel more cheerful and she was right. I've seen her give impromptu makeovers to charity shop staff – she once came to my house once and painted my furniture green and yellow.*

*Emily knows all about nature. When you go for a walk with her, she points out nature and quotes facts. It's like she's part of another world with its own language. Another world that is there all the time, but only people with LSD eyes like Emily can point it out to us.*

*Emily can cook a meal out of anything she finds in a cupboard and feed the whole street with a minute's notice. She has an open-door policy and will let you in and treat you like a queen or king if you have a good heart and good stories to tell. She brings people up. You cannot be sad around Emily for long. Her joy is contagious.*

*But don't mistake her for being soft. She is tall and strong like a warrior woman and takes no shit. She has an assertiveness about her that lets you know she will not suffer fools.*

**Toria Garbutt**
*(Yorkshire based writer and celebrated spoken word artist)*

*Just like you deciding to pick up this book, Emily came into my life at exactly the right time. Stars aligned and we were brought together by a wedding while our own marriages and theologies were falling apart. Mutually navigating the unravelling was a beautiful feminist act of caretaking each other. But I do believe Emily brings that same non-judgemental compassion to the stranger on the bus, the old man walking by the lake, and the cashier at the market. To come across her path is to be brought in to her colourful ever-expanding universe where everything is possible and too much is just right. This book will give you an opportunity to sit on the banks of her babbling brook of a narrative and reflect. By the end you might realise that you too now have a new best friend.*

**Andrea Bibee**
*(Oregon's enigmatic doula to the stars and mother of most holy mischief)*

*Without music to decorate it, time is just a bunch of boring production deadlines or dates by which bills must be paid.[1]*

*Frank Zappa wrote that.*

*Of course, there are more ways to decorate life than just music. Frank was looking through the lens of his area of expertise and inspiration. Musical communion with his carefully-curated bandmates took him far beyond the limits of regular existence. Forty years later, the musical concepts and experiences that he and his band discovered are shining monuments to what a human artist can become a part of – with the right combination of discipline and discernment.*

*The experience of knowing the accomplished artist – and now author – Emily Garcés is like that for me. Time spent with Emily feels like being part of an existential band on a par with Zappa's adventurers: a day caving followed by a bizarre encounter with an eccentric-karaoke-singing-antique-shop-owner, an impromptu cocktail evening with an author of a book about sex addition and a lover of urban agriculture visiting from Philadelphia – I always come away feeling greater from the experience of having mingled with her energy, her love of the genuine, her embrace of the unknown, her penchant for kind-hearted mischief, her fearless engagement with strangers – I could go on.*

*No less impressive is her commitment to a never-ending search for a greater integrity, and to the cultivation of the divinity with which we are all seeded as human beings, should we only choose to encourage its germination.*

**Paul Jackson**
*(world renowned mariner and Canada's ambassador of connoisseurship)*

*I found Emily by searching for the word artist on the travel website Workaway and lived with her family for a few weeks near the beginning of my international year of creative living. When I arrived, she took one look at me and said, "We will not be doing any cleaning this week, we will play, and we will record podcast episodes."*

*Emily's life is a work of art. She has a current of creativity rushing through her that not only fuels her whimsical painting and poetically hilarious storytelling, but also sparks her connection with the world around her, inspiring her to rescue a family of marginalized swans in an IKEA bag from the pond behind her home and orchestrate an impromptu speed-dating event at a local pub that accidentally transforms into an evening of profound healing. Emily has a gift of truly seeing people and welcoming them to their lives, as if to say: Hello, human being! I see you and all the things you try to hide from the world–those are the things that make you special and interesting. Let's play!*

*Emily's writing is refreshing and delicious because she lives by her own rule of saying yes! to whatever will make the best story–whether it is hitchhiking with drunken nuns or inviting a gaggle of internet daters to participate in a riveting conversation about spirituality. She trusts herself to live with her heart wide open in the moment, in the rich, textured, colourful movie that is her life, and invites us all to do the same.*

**Katie Barbaro**

*(stand-up comedian and host of the podcast Showing Up Messy)*

*I first met Emily at a small gathering of LGBTQIA folks, I'm not sure how we'd describe ourselves? Post-Christian, emergent Church, community of faith, or church rejects. Emily blended in just fine. Before I could drop her at the railway station, she had taken me for a strawberry beer and recorded a podcast episode with me in my car. The sheer energy, honesty and love that poured from her caught me by surprise, I'd thought her young enough to be my daughter, but her wisdom and humour showed the heart and mind of someone twice my age.*

*I have been transgender fifty-five years, all my conscious life. I've been a stumbling disciple of Jesus for nearly forty years. I've watched churches spew out those who don't fit its laws and beliefs. I'm aching, longing to embrace a healthier body of Christ. On our meeting Emily told me that my voice needs to be heard, and I needed to hear that. I've lived my life with the homeless and the down-and-outs, the addicts, and the poor. It's who I am. It's where I meet Jesus. We both share a desire to water the wastelands where the marginalised are exiled, to draw them into the warmth, for the good of society as a whole, not just for those individuals. Emily doesn't so much talk about faith as live it, from her fragile vulnerability flows a radiance, compassion and magnetism that challenges and inspires. Behind her gift of words is a love, life and fire I find liberating, affirming and life giving.*

**Chrissie Chevasutt**

*(lover of Jesus, racer of bicycles, author of Transgender Disciple)*

———◇◇◇———

*Foreword*

Hitchhiking with Drunken Nuns happened because of a missed bus that left us stranded on the wrong side of The Andes. There have been a lot of missed buses in my life: missed religious buses, missed relationship buses, missed education buses, missed creative buses, missed opportunity of my life buses. I used to get angry. I used to mourn a missed bus as if someone had died. With time I learned to shift my energy and the anger lessened. Yes, I still mourn a little when I miss one, but not in such a way that I stop being open to the life that comes after it. Slowly, I learned not to sit waiting painfully for a new bus, that takes the same route. I learned to open myself to all manner of routes, all manner of vehicles, and all manner of slightly drunken travelling companions.

It hurts when our spiritual journey is forced to take a route other than the one we had planned.

It hurts when a relationship does not follow the pattern that we prescribed for it.

It hurts when our community presents differently to the one we looked for.

It hurts when something disrupts the direction that our creative project was taking.

It hurts when our life is not the life we thought we wanted.

But there is hope. Not hope that everything will be resolved – but hope that waits undiscovered right at the heart of all those unresolved things. This is a book about that hope – but it is also a book about the painstakingly long, and often uncomfortable, trip it took to get me there.

It is a book of two halves: The first is a half of religious unravelling and unanswered questions. The second is a half of ravelling (which in some ways is just a more cheerfully tangled way to say further unravelling). This second half looks at what happens to a person who chooses to keep an open heart and embrace creativity after the walls of institution and borrowed-belief collapse. It is a book full of the joy of missed buses, failed relationships, unconventional communities, and artistic shortcuts.

Sometimes your travel plans fail you when you are in a remote part of Patagonia, and you are forced to hitchhike with drunken nuns to get home. Sometimes you start a clumsy conversation over the aubergines in a supermarket and end up making a friend for life. Sometimes you are pregnant and panicking in Venezuela before you start to doubt your belief in religion enough to open up space for mystery. Sometimes it is not until after a story ends that you notice there was a story there at all. Sometimes it is not until after a marriage has stalled and broken down that you realise that the roadside where it has left you can become a better place entirely if you stick out your thumb and trust. Sometimes false starts are the only real way you can begin something. Sometimes the most beautiful weddings are the ones in which the groom has just been diagnosed with cancer. Sometimes you make a stupid mistake when you are on the verge of finishing a painting, but you acknowledge it, and do not try too hard to cover it up – and it becomes the most beautiful part of the piece. Sometimes you are halfway through writing a book and you feel like a fraud – you are scared that you will regret half the things you write, scared that half of them make no sense, scared that you will accidentally hurt those you love, scared because for every one thing that you know – there are a thousand things you do not. Then suddenly you realise that the things you do not know, are worth so much more than the things you do. You realise that you do not want to give people another self-help book, because the messiness of the moment with its mountains of mistakes is the best gift there is to give.

You think – well, what have I got to lose?
And you reply – nothing that I have not lost already.

Self-help culture is damaging because it emphasises the distance between where you are and where you should be. Your head gets stuck in the space between those two things. Hope is tied to an imaginary future and severed from the messiness of the moment. You dream of a spirituality that can be neatly contained, of creative art-forms that can be mastered, and of relationships that fit pre-scribed patterns. What happens when life does not fit this formula? Chaos that's what – terrifying, infuriating, sometimes exhilarating, and occasionally wonderful chaos, but that chaos is not a dream. It is not imaginary. It is where you are now. It is who you are now. It is the truth. Yes – this truth may be hard to handle, but it is sin-cere enough to free you from the false promise of answers and loyal enough to join you in your questions – saying *hey, maybe the point is not to be complete, maybe the point is to be completely alive.*

By the end of this book I am not the same person I was at the beginning. Whether or not that is a good thing is up to you to decide. My story does not have the happy ending that I so very much wanted it to have. In the process of writing I realised that endings do not exist, and that happy is not a destination. But oh – what a journey we are on – peaked with elation and spiked with pain, crammed with wonder and surprise. There will be times when we wish we could turn back, but we stick out our thumbs in a tired act of defiance. Then the nuns arrive. Responding to our open hearts. Grinning with divine drunkenness. When we feel lost and alone there is always a creative way to get from A to B – and the best thing is that A and B are only the first two letters of the alphabet.

In 1949 Joseph Campbell wrote a book called *The Hero with a Thousand Faces*[2] in which he points out that (because of an inbuilt archetypal template) the same story resurfaces across world mythology: The hero is called from the known into the unknown, faces challenges and temptations, death, rebirth and transformation – before returning to the known world bearing gifts to share with others. The role of women in this journey often feels limited to that of prize or companion. I grew up reading and watching these stories and often felt excluded. I did not want to be a princess waiting to be rescued, but I did not want to be the prince either. I wanted something else. Without knowing it, I longed for a journey into the archetype of the dynamic feminine. I wanted to embrace the female counterpart to the hero's journey. The hero is often depicted as returning from his journey with new information that strengthens the structure of society. My hunger has mostly been for information that will loosen this structure and move us towards fluidity and oneness.

We are in an age when the new Boadiceas, Annie Londonderrys, Joan of Arcs, Dorothy Lawrences and Maya Angelous will not be swept under the dark carpet of history. It is an age in which seeds dropped by forgotten heroes will sprout out at impossible angles. An age when reverse narratives will become learning curves. An age when feminine energy will implode even the American Dream, breaking up its components and sharing them out like the miracle of bread amongst thousands.

Mine is a journey of unknowing – culminating in a great unbecoming. Like any great journey it is without end, folding back in on itself, a symbol of infinity like the seasons: leaves budding green as soon as winter turns its back, only to wither in apparent defeat when winter faces them again. Dynamic Masculine, and Dynamic Feminine heroes return with arms full of gifts which provide the flow of our overlapping and interweaving journeys with vital new energy. I have poured many of the things I have received along the way into this book, in the hope that you might be able to fashion a few of them into tools that will help you on your own journey. My word of warning is for you not to assume that you know how your journey will end. I have come to realise that it is sometimes the princess who needs to rescue the dragon from the well-meaning (but deluded) hero.

I had a dream the night before I started writing this book:

*A broken butterfly fumbles its way around the kitchen floor. I have been observing it for a while, days, weeks maybe. Because of its beauty I long for it to live despite the impossibility of its situation. Someone comes through the door and I see it slip out past them. Cold and dark outside, my heart sinks. No chance for it. Then I see something strange; its damaged wings open and it begins to fly. Pinks and golds and yellows in the night sky. Oh, it is a moth not a butterfly – it is made for the darkness, it shines there. I do not squeal with joy – I almost cry with it. I see something else. A huge exotic green and gold moth. They are drawn together, as if by a light they each are making. Others appear, each of them also generating their own light. Then I glance up and become aware of a giant hippo floating in the sky on helium, huge and smiling. And I say "oh, you are beautiful. What sort of a creature are you?" And the hippo replies in a voice too deep and too profound for it to be audible.*

I know that hippos are angry creatures, and that they are fierce. But this giant hippo is tethered like a balloon – as if her anger has been harnessed for good. At the time of writing this I am feeling a lot of anger at various political and world events. This is an anger that I want to harness. The hate in the world has been given an outrageous voice – I want the love in the world to have a voice which is equally outrageous. I do not care how crazy it gets. I want my voice (and yours) to be part of it. For many years I have had a tattoo of a butterfly on my back. One of its wings is damaged but it still flies. We are all of us broken, but we are capable of greatness, and together we are capable of generating an impossible amount of light.

Although I still do not know what it is that the hippo is saying, I awake knowing that his words are the next line in the song of who I am – a key phrase in the song of Emily. It's a song I hum sometimes when it is deathly quiet. Why should you sit and listen as I sing this song of mine? Why should you lend me your ear as I recall these experiences? Why should I become one more voice when there are so many voices that buzz around us vying for our attention? I listen to these voices too – I listen to intellectual debates, I learn long words, I listen to poetry, I listen to music, I repeat other people's words back to myself and hold them close to my heart like a comfort blanket. Though there are times when it is so quiet that I cannot hear other people's words, so quiet that the only voice I can hear is my own. I forget that I can generate my own words in the same way that the broken moth could generate her own light. Like so many people, I sit, and I listen to other people singing songs about themselves. I do not think that I am worthy of a song of my own. That is changing now. I am writing my own song in the faith that it will inspire you to listen to your own voice in the deep silence – and that you will start to hum the song of yourself – quietly at first, and then with the full capacity of your lungs.

Writing my song starts with this book – and I am terrified, and embarrassed, and deeply ashamed of a lot of my story, and of much of those seven years that I spent on the mission field. But these are the sentiments that I am choosing to embrace – I will not turn my back on them anymore – I accept them as my own. I choose to open my heart to you and to the whole messy truth of it all. I choose to be my authentic slightly drunken self. My door is open to you if you wish to join me for the journey.

# *Introduction*

A slightly odd sort of young child is created when raised in the countryside with very little television and without siblings of their own age. That child spends a lot of time wandering around their own head. If they ever process externally it is usually with animals or imaginary friends.

I had invisible dinosaurs that I carried around in the open palms of my hands, and a cat called Sophie who I took with me everywhere – so she would be able to accompany me to heaven if I died suddenly. I looked at the world so intently that I saw things that others could not see. Sometimes it shimmered and became so translucent that I could float right through it and spend time in an overlapping reality. Once it snapped so sharply back into focus that I saw a tiny shrew being chased by a cat in the long grass through the kitchen window. I ran out to catch her, letting her bite the insides of my cupped hands as I released her safely in a neighbour's orchard. The pain did not matter, because the freedom I gave her was my freedom.

The rough sloping field behind my house was the backdrop for imagined adventures. I hid from angry Welsh farmers in dens that I thought made me invisible. Weeing in streams and pooing under large flat stones so I did not have to go back inside until teatime. I sat astride the curved back of my favourite tree like it was a battle-ready horse, gazing solemnly out along the Welsh coastline, envisaging approaching pirates coming to hunt the plastic treasure trinkets I buried under rocks. I dreamed of future adventures. Not of waiting captive in a tower, but of cutting through forests with a sword in my hand, anticipating meeting a dragon and saving it from the prince who is too busy imagining enemies to notice me.

As I grow older the anticipation of such adventures never fades, but it does become more realistic. The planes of fantasy and reality continue to overlap so closely that castle-crowned peaks break through at the most ordinary of moments. The magic is less frequent and less prolonged, it is further away, but still present. My life becomes an ongoing attempt to reach through the thin curtain that divides the secular and the sacred, an attempt to reach through the cold chest of the mundane in order to grasp at the mythical heart of the magic. We are heroes in the adventure story of our own creating, and even though sightings of mystical beasts might be rare, and unexplored lands might have been tamed for property development – our story can never be devoid of significance. Our story is not dictated by the giant road map that society thrusts into our hands, but instead by the quiet voice of the child inside us who is young enough to remember the oceans of love she inhabited before she was born.

I remember standing on a low wall at the edge of the playground of my Welsh speaking Primary School with cardboard wings taped to my back. I jump and run – feeling like the buzzing they make in the sudden rush of air is them activating ready for take-off. I was somehow born with the knowledge that there is another realm we can reach as soon as we learn to fly. I want the rushing clouds of activity to stop for a second, so everyone will be able to glimpse the stars above us. Stars that my deep memories of night-time project onto the blueness. I want everyone to sense the river of providence running underneath it all.

The first person I fell in love with was my next-door neighbour. We were both very young children with very old souls. Despite the brooding presence of her father, which loomed from his armchair in the corner, Dawn's soft glow drew me from my terraced house to hers. I spent the days sipping sugary tea from a glossy brown mug. Enveloped by the warmth of her mother Marie's Liverpudlian accent as she called me *Pooh Bear* and scrubbed at the L shaped birthmark on my forehead thinking it was dirt. I cannot pronounce my Rs, so I called her *Aunty Wee.* She gave me a Mars Bar once and I made it last a week. I did not get such things at home. My own mother fed me on homemade rye bread and sunflower seeds (which she said protected me from the radiation reaching Wales from Chernobyl). At night I longed to scratch a hole from my house to Dawn's to hold her hand in the darkness. I have a photograph of us on the shoreline, hugging each other so fiercely that you see me wanting to disappear into her soul, to sink into the ocean with her and return to that watery place of primordial unity. I looked into her eyes and saw myself for the first time, truly becoming aware that I existed. That space between us became for moments like a shortcut to the great unreachable otherness on the other side of the universe.

When I feel old and tired, I return to this six-year-old self. I stand again at the cusp of life – at the bottom of a mountain, at the bow of a ship. I see myself with new eyes. I start the whole adventure again, as if it is for the first time. Parts of the journey need to be faced alone, but company is necessary too. We need guides to act as mirrors to our humanity – sometimes it is hard to see ourselves with new eyes without the mirror of another person. We need to stick out our thumbs when we are tired of walking by ourselves and trust that the next car to stop will be the right one. If that car happens to be full of drunken holidaying nuns, you can be sure that the road ahead will be paved with a wonderfully cracked form of spirituality.

A new age is dawning, and if we have to hitchhike with drunken nuns in order to be there in time for the sunrise – then so be it. We are in an era of post-Christendom and are desperately holding on to old religious models. We are in a post-industrial society that still insists on squeezing its children through an outdated factory school system. We are living in communities that we have not noticed are there because the nuclear community we are waiting for is one that no longer exists. The problem is that our dreams are outdated; we are climbing towards a summit that has been completely eroded away by time. We need new dreams, but first we need to let go of the old ones. That is as hard for us as it was for Miss Havisham to get out of her once beautiful wedding dress. For such a task we need something that is a grade stronger than our usual brand of courage. Danish Pastor Kaj Munk says, "Our task today is recklessness.[3]" We need a holy disregard for the norms that society says are acceptable.

Hitchhiking is exactly the sort of risky thing that we are not supposed to do. I am speaking metaphorically – about the act of believing in the serendipity of coincidence – about the possible danger involved in trusting the goodness of others. What if we get lost? What if they hurt us? American author and former pastor, Rob Bell says, "Risk is where the life is." That is why we are drawn to it in the way love draws a person into a relationship, even though they are terrified it will end badly.

## Open-hearted Creativity

There are two things we need in order to make our relationship with risk a healthy one: *Open-heartedness* and *Creativity*. Open-heartedness is the fertile ground needed for any genuine human connection to grow. Creativity is the dance with which we bend to avoid blows and jump to reach greater heights. Together they do not provide us with fail-safe protection from risk, but they do give us a spirit-enhancing way to live with risk as part of our lives. This is a battle fought primarily in the territory of the heart. Such a strange muscle. Armour suffocates it and prevents it from getting the exercise it needs. A heart not exposed to risk might curl up on the sofa and die an early death.

Sometimes – like stepping onto a dance floor at a school disco – the first step is the hardest. Sometimes you need an invitation and a hand to hold. I extend mine. Here is the permission to dance your heart out no matter how bad the music. Your dance will not be the same as my dance (if you have seen me dance, you will know that is a good thing). I do not advise you to try to imitate the way I live my life, but I would advise that you try hard to dance your own dance without worrying about what others are thinking. I will take you to the dance floor – the rest is up to you.

To give permission to your creativity is to allow yourself to speak, and then to allow yourself to admit that you have a voice worth listening to – because you do. To give permission to your open-heartedness is to allow yourself to love, and then to allow yourself to admit that you are worthy of love – because you are. Receiving permission to be both open-hearted and creative, is that which will give your love a voice.

Patterns exist within patterns and journeys exist within journeys. A heart open wide enough absorbs the creative blueprints behind the mind of the universe. The characteristics that we give that mind are the characteristics we choose for ourselves. Permission to be both open-hearted and creative is given when we grant the same qualities to the architect of the universe which we then inhabit. We – of course – do not get to change the actual nature of that unspeakable mystery, but we get to change the metaphors we use to pin our own meaning to the parts of it we choose to imagine. The artistic process needed to create the metaphors and stories to describe the sort of creator you imagine created you can be long, and extremely arduous.

It requires an insane amount of patience.

And a good sense of humour.

# Finding an Open-hearted Creative God

*"At the end of the day, 'God' is a makeshift*
*term, a stop-gap: a way of clearing the throat*
*(as Leonard Cohen might say) before attempting,*
*once again, to utter the unutterable."*

*– Dave Tomlinson (Black Sheep and Prodigals[4])*

As I write this, I am simultaneously having a WhatsApp conversation with my Canadian atheist friend Paul who is on a boat rescuing refugees who have come from Libya on a raft. We have got onto the subject of enlightenment. Paul is wondering whether the trend for mindfulness is a way to create yet another self-induced high. We both agree that some of the self-proclaimed enlightened ones have an aura of smugness that can be hard to penetrate. Paul says that in a world made only of flowers there would be no rock and roll – and surely that would be unbearable. I agree. All my favourite people are a little bit lost and a little bit broken. Knowing that gives me permission to stop pretending. It stops me longing for a religion that will make me whole and shiny and makes me long for an inclusive community where our weakness becomes what knits us together.

I cannot define my faith any more than I can define Christianity itself. Christianity, like my own journey, is not over yet and it is hard to summarise what is not complete. I would currently describe myself as a Christian Mystic. Christianity is the framework I was given to construct my world on. There are other frameworks, there are other worlds. I do not think that mine is better than anyone else's. It just makes sense for me to start with the broken pieces I have got, rather than smashing up a different belief system to make new pieces – I like to recycle. Jesus, as the religion's central figure, is someone whose boundary-breaking love also smashed things up a little – and I cannot help but be drawn to that. Mysticism for me is a way of experiencing the absolute freeing truth of God without investing too much in futile attempts to frame the unspeakable wonder with words. I see the space that my knowledge inhabits as being a tiny dot on a huge web of learning, I want it to expand outwards and inwards rather than to head out in a predetermined direction.

The Franciscan Father Richard Rohr asks us to imagine three boxes: Order, Disorder, and Reorder[5]. A more Conservative belief system tends to keep us in the box labelled *Order*, progressives and liberals move to the box of *Disorder*, and often stay there. Rohr says that the great myths and religions of the world document the journey to the third box as *the normal path of transformation.*

It was the radical Irish theologian Peter Rollins who introduced me to the meaning of the word ravel. I always thought that the word meant simply the opposite of unravel. The dictionary says that this unusual verb can mean both *tangle* and *untangle* simultaneously. As threads come unwoven from a cloth, they become tangled on each other. For me, it is this word that opens up the paradoxical possibility of occupying the last two boxes at the same time. Some recovering faith addicts refer to a deconstruction and a reconstruction of religion. I think they are the same thing.

My faith has become a space where, in the same instance, I can fall apart and be put back together. A space where I can forgive and be forgiven. A space where I can be completely lost and completely found. Completely broken and completely whole. It is a space where pain and joy can coexist without being enemies, where comedy and tragedy are two sides of the same coin. A space where answers and questions are part of the same utterance. The creative flow extending from these absurd couplings gives love space to stretch its limbs and be comfortable, allowing us to know deeply that the very air we breathe is the unspeakable name of God.

But the journey through the boxes of Order, Disorder, and Reorder begins with the first box – and maybe that is the way it always has to be. I spend the first half of this book trying to figure out how to get out of it – or how to make myself shrink enough so I can fit inside it more comfortably.

CHAPTER 1

*Born Again*

I become a Christian at the age of five in a children's club called Christian Endeavour. The club is held in a small hall, one of the few weekly events in the tiny Welsh village of Llanbedr. A well-meaning lady called Linda prays a prayer of Christian commitment and I repeat it back to her line by line:

*Dear Lord Jesus,*
*I thank you for loving me so much*
*that you spread out your arms on the cross*
*to tell me just how big your love for me is.*
*I choose to accept you as my personal Lord and Saviour.*
*Thank you for the grace I do not deserve.*
*Please forgive me for all the bad things that I have done*
*and give me the strength to follow you each and every day.*
*Amen.*

I associate that prayer with the memory of a small red slide clipped onto a wooden climbing frame, and the plastic taste of a cup half-full of over-diluted orange squash.

My parents have not been Christians for long themselves. We live in a small cottage, with two rooms downstairs and two bedrooms upstairs. We have two dogs, two cats, and I have two much older brothers from my mother's first marriage. The house is a middle terrace and is sandwiched between the ocean and the foothills of the Snowdonia mountains. In the hills up above us, is a Christian Mountain Centre called The Ranch. I am too young to remember but I have heard it said that they offer my family food that is surplus to their needs and slowly draw my parents into their small Christian community.

We leave Wales when I am seven and these close neighbourly connections are much grieved. We move to a town called New Mills, situated to the south of Manchester and to the West of the Peak District National Park. New Mills, although still plenty rural, feels like a big city compared to the remoteness and closeness of Llanbedr.

## Butterfly in a Box

*The field that yielded six of my years*
*Is reduced to a postage stamp, beyond which*
*The Ocean waves through the fogged-up window,*
*A square of blue,*
*Like the closed box I clutch with the butterfly brooch,*
*A parting gift from my best friend, a souvenir*
*Of fading innocence.*
*I am so young, I have no idea*
*That I belong to the ocean,*
*That it is the map of my freedom,*
*That the land will surround me like an early grave*
*As I am driven from Wales to Manchester*

*In the back of a Ford Fiesta.*
*They know what is best for me,*
*You will like your new school,*
*There is a park near our house,*
*With a see-saw and a paddling pool.*
*I am so young, I have no idea*
*That there is no playground like a field*
*And no pool like the sea.*

My parents soon reach for the security of the local church. New Mills Christian Fellowship is a denomination-free congregation located in old Wesleyan Chapel half way down a steep winding road called High Street. The man in charge is someone called Phil, but there are two other men, Brian and John, who also carry a fair amount of responsibility. Phil is balding with thick glasses; he smells of sawdust from the woodwork classes he teaches. John always wears brown jumpers that look itchy, all his socks are also brown, so they are never odd. John also wears glasses and has a large red beard. Both Phil and John drive Volvo estates. John's Volvo is brown. Both have extra seats fitted into the boot. I love these seats because they face backwards. Both Phil and John have two daughters with whom I am friends. After church I often sit in one of the backwards facing seats and go to one of their homes for Sunday Lunch. We play hide and seek and make *Jesus loves YOU* bookmarks which I sell at the back of church – until I am asked to stop because people are giving me the money instead of putting it in the offering.

Brian is different to Phil and John because he drives a Mitsubishi Space Wagon. It has lots of seats that he can adjust to different positions to make space for children and musical equipment. Brian always wears a grey jumper with a faint fair-isle pattern in light blue, it looks less itchy than John's and matches his sofas perfectly. Brian is the coolest of the three because his hair grows up a little at the front and out a little at the back. He also has a rainbow guitar strap and is in a Christian rock band called *The Predators*, where he plays a self-made synthesiser with three keyboards stacked one on top of the other. Brian is the father of my new best friend Lorna, and they live only two streets away.

The Church service starts at ten o'clock every Sunday. The congregation is always the same. Dennis, who has large ears and a kind face and knows how to make beautiful wooden chairs. Bonus, an old man who I never really understand because of the strength of his Derbyshire accent. Gaynor, a young woman with down-syndrome who hugs everyone with an iron grip. Gaynor is also the church's most enthusiastic singer. Elsie, who for decades seems to remain at about the age of ninety. Sometimes Elsie falls asleep during the service and snores loudly; when we wake her gently, she earnestly informs us that she has been praying. Our favourite is Lilian, an old lady with short curly hair who always gives us sweets after the service. I especially remember the taste of lemon polos, a taste made better because of its long anticipation throughout the service. Lilian understands the importance of enticing children to church and keeping them there.

The meeting starts with praise songs which have actions. We stretch our fingers skyward and imagine how much taller we would have to be to reach God. Forty minutes of worship songs are followed by twenty minutes of preaching. I have always been a fussy digester of music. I could deliberately drown myself in a shallow song, and swim for miles in something deeper. I have a sense that Christian worship music can be treated like the Bible: all the worst bits get repeated, the best bits ignored, and songs and verses that start out OK become intolerable because of misuse or overuse.

Graham Kendrick is the Godfather of Christian Worship music, and the height of his reign is in the eighties. The song that is sung until it becomes threadbare is *Shine Jesus Shine*, it was written in 1987, a year before we moved to New Mills. This is how it starts:

*Lord, the light of your love is shining*
*In the midst of the darkness, shining*
*Jesus, Light of the world, shine upon us*
*Set us free by the truth you now bring us*[6]

Here is another Kendrick song. It is not one that I ever heard sung at my church. The lyrics are quite thought provoking in places. Although it does still end with the classic formula: Jesus dies in our place and under the weight of our sins.

*How much do you think you are worth?*
*Is a rich man worth more than a poor man?*
*A stranger worth less than a friend?*
*Is a baby worth more than an old man?*
*Your beginning worth more than your end?*
*Is a president worth more than his assassin?*
*Does your value decrease with your crime?*
*Like when Christ took the place of Barabbas*

*Would you say he was wasting his time?*

I think one of the reasons why that song is not sung is because the gospel message it contains is not clear enough. The bit about the president and the assassin is especially confusing. It is important that we do not forget for a moment how simple Christianity is. We needed to keep the basic formula in mind at all times. If we stop singing about it, we might completely forget that we are Christians. I first learn the gospel formula with the prayer that I pray when I am five, and it has been playing on repeat ever since. I wonder if any brain would be capable of questioning such a message with this degree of exposure.

Here are some of the songs I remember best. They must be the ones we sing every week. I am going to write them out so you get a sense of what my Sunday mornings feel like.

*There is a redeemer*
*Jesus, God's own Son*
*Precious Lamb of God, Messiah*
*Holy One[7]*

*Lord I lift your name on high*
*Lord I love to sing your praises*
*I'm so glad you are in my life*
*I'm so glad you came to save us[8]*

The Gospel of these songs is based on the theory of penal substitutionary atonement (PSA). The theory was a relative newcomer to the Christian faith – beginning to evolve around the 11th century after Christ. I was told that *being saved* means that Jesus has suffered on the cross so that we will never have to suffer again. God is angry at us because of the sin that Adam and Eve introduce in the Garden of Eden. He takes that anger out on His Son so we can go free. God so hated what we'd done to the world that He kills his only-begotten-son. It means we can spend every Sunday in Church revelling in how easily we have been let off the hook. *Phew* – we say, wiping collective beads of sweat off our foreheads with the backs of our hands, before proceeding to burst into another song of repetitive gratitude.

*Jesus we celebrate Your victory*
*Jesus we revel in Your love*

...

*And in his presence our problems disappear*
*Our hearts responding to his love*[9]

Being told that *our problems disappear* in His presence puts a lot of pressure on a person. If I still have problems does that mean that God is far away? That His presence is not near? I only have seconds to think about these questions before the next song starts and I drown again in the sea of everyone else's unquestioning gratitude:

*Father God, I wonder how I*
*managed to exist without the*
*knowledge of your parenthood*
*and Your loving care.*
*Now I am your son I am adopted in your family*[10]

God is a Father. I am his son. I try hard to squeeze my feminine soul into a patriarchal mould. Sometimes though – sometimes I wonder to God about other things. Sometimes I leave the script. What if Jesus is supposed to be followed, as well as worshipped? What if the cross is a way in rather than a way out? What if we were to embrace suffering rather than deny it? What if the cross demonstrates the painfully non-violent response that we could replicate when faced with a suffering world? What if that act is about His empathy with our pain, rather than His liberation of us from it? But I do not wonder for long; these songs are so confident and so sure of themselves. We sing the Rich Mullins song *Our God is an Awesome God*[11], but we never sing his song *Hold me Jesus*, not in public, at least. It opens with the verse:

> *Well, sometimes my life just don't make sense at all*
> *When the mountains look so big,*
> *And my faith just seems so small*[12]

Looking up at people's faces as they sing any song but this one, I get a sense that they are singing these songs so confidently to make up for a lack of confidence somewhere deep within. The place you learn to take home with you and not get out at church – a place you only examine when it is late at night and you are alone, before putting it away and pretending that you hadn't.

The psalms that we quote from The Bible are chosen in much the same way. Even though most of the psalms are those of lament, containing lines like: *For my soul is full of trouble and my life draws near the grave* (Psalm 88). We only ever really read the ones that present a more cheerful formula for life.

Although I see all the same people at church every week, I feel I never really know many of them (except Jim. I go downstairs for Sunday school early once and catch him banging his head on the wall. I always liked Jim). Although the Gospel has already been stretched to its thinnest point, the children still leave at the height of the service to receive an even simpler version of it at Sunday school. Jesus is a flat character, a cartoon sketch that I colour in, staying inside the lines.

It is not a perfect church, but it is our church, and we did love it. I would like to imagine that it is neither better nor worse than any other eighties evangelical British congregation. But soon New Mills Christian Fellowship hits a wall. A literal one. There is a large crack in the external structure that we cannot afford to mend, so the church is taken over by Christians from a neighbouring town. The two congregations merge. I am about ten by now, and I am outraged (as were the other children). We run around writing *this building is the property of New Mills Christian Fellowship I.D.F.T.* on scraps of paper which we jam into crevices. To no avail – a sign is erected outside which reads *Christian Revival Church*. We are no longer denomination-free – we are Assemblies of God.

The heat starts to pick up. The worship band gets bigger; the back room opening to create a stage to accommodate them. There has not been a stage before. Just Brian in his grey jumper, standing politely at the front with a guitar and a solitary keyboard. The sermons are also being elevated; they are now longer and louder. There is a new woman called Margaret sitting at the front (where she can position song lyrics on the overhead projector) pronouncing "that's right!" after everything that is preached. She punches her arms upwards and outwards very suddenly during any worship song that stirs her spontaneously. It is best not to be sitting near her at these moments.

Despite these changes, the very same Gospel is being preached, though there is even more pressure than before to make sure that we understand it correctly. A list of membership requirements is written out and my father is made to feel increasingly uncomfortable for believing in science. I do not think that children can become members even if they want to, so I am not overly concerned. I do, however, feel that I have failed somewhat regarding the gospel; I cannot quite work out how it applies to me.

I know that the word Gospel means Good News. That our sin separates us from God, and that Jesus has been punished on our behalf so that we can be saved from God's judgement. I just find it hard to understand how my pre-Christian five-year-old self is so radically different from the person I am now. I do not feel like I have been saved from much.

Even at my young age I have already read a lot of books. I mostly read the books that are commonly found around my house: stories of Christian conversion. One of my favourites is called *Run Baby Run*[13], the story of Nicky Cruz, who is born in Puerto Rico to abusive parents who practice witchcraft. At the age of fifteen they send him to live with his brother in New York. It is not long before he flees to the streets where he becomes a member of a gang called the Mau Maus. After six months he had risen to be their leader. A preacher tries to lead the gang to Jesus and Nicky responds by slapping him and threatening to kill him. But the preacher is persistent and soon the promise of God's love and forgiveness becomes something that he cannot resist. Nicky quickly becomes as committed to Christianity as he has been to his gang. He must have remained committed because I hear him preach in the UK thirty years after his book is written.

It is easy for Nicky. He can walk up to any stranger on the street and tell them his story and they would be unable to deny God's ability to transform lives. It is harder for me. How can I spread a Gospel that has not transformed me?

I find the only solution available.

To increase the contrast between *the before* and *the after*, I will have to make *the after* a lot more impressive. That way maybe it will not matter if my testimony is not as good as Nicky's. This objective results in quite an interesting late childhood.

I attend as many Christian meetings and events as I can. Sometimes staying up to pray into the small hours. I take it all very seriously. I have prayer sticks which I pound on the floor and Bible cassettes which I listen to on my Walkman, whilst the other kids listen to Oasis. I sometimes wake up crying at the thought of all my school friends going to Hell. I think that if God is real, and the salvation of the world really does hang in balance, then the least I can do is to dedicate my life to it.

I remember one day surprisingly clearly. I am at an Assemblies of God conference at Lancaster University with my Church, I must have been about fourteen. I remember two events which happen in the main auditorium.

My mother goes up onto the stage to respond to an alter call as
I sit and watch. I see her tell one of the prayer team that she wants
God to heal her leg which is causing her pain. I watch them pray
for her and then half push her forward to test the results. *Run!* They
tell her, *run!* She looks hesitant, but they are not really giving her
a choice. She runs. The applause which floods the auditorium is
deafening. There is something I know, that the congregation does
not –my mother can sprint short distances. The problem with her
leg is that the pain means she cannot walk for long without stopping
for regular rests.

I glance behind me during the same service and notice a young
man wearing a baseball cap enter to stand awkwardly at the back
of the room. The preacher has also noticed him. *Young man! This is
the House of the Lord. You have shown disrespect to God by not removing
your hat.* The room turns to look at him. I look down, ashamed. The
disrespect shown to the vulnerable young man is far greater in my
opinion. I regret not following him as he leaves the building still
wearing his cap.

That afternoon I take my Bible and walk quickly away from
the concrete walls of the University. I find a wooded area and lean
back against a tree, letting the sunlight dry out the bad weather
from my thoughts. I sit with The Book open in my hand, feeling
its weight and tapping its leather skin with my finger. I wonder if
the words trapped between its pages feel like I felt inside that auditorium. I wonder if they are as alive as the world around me. It
is a beautiful day. A rabbit skips in the far distance. Wild flowers
buckle in the slight breeze. Woodpigeons call and answer (one of my
favourite sounds in all the world). A thought comes to me with such

a strength that it leaves my lips as a whispered prayer: *God, it is so beautiful being so close to nature, I wish it were possible to feel even closer to your creation.* Then. At this exact moment. There is a noise above me that sounds like the squawk of a magpie and a squirrel falls out of the tree and lands squarely on my head. It scrambles quickly away, glancing once over its shoulder, as if also struggling to believe what had just happened. I wonder if squirrels are instruments in the hands of God, if they work for him like the Elves do for Father Christmas. I laugh for about three hours straight, which is fine in this sort of Christian environment – people can just assume that I have been touched by the Holy Spirit.

C H A P T E R   2

*The Aaron Emails*

My Christian journey continues to give me a lot to process. Conflicting thoughts often jostle around so quickly that my head heats up with the friction. I have some close friends in the church who I talk to, but none who can handle the sheer volume of topics that I need to discuss. Then, shortly after the internet has been invented, I meet Aaron. I am joking around with a friend and choose his email from a Christian website. She dares me to write to him out of the blue and ask him to marry me. I am seventeen and he is a sixteen-year-old American from Kansas City. We email each other daily for years. I thought that all record of this had been lost, until recently when the Australian living in my Caravan discovers a suitcase full of printouts in the attic.

Here are some of those emails.

Aaron,

Here is my quote from Grapes of Wrath for the day:

*And from this first "we" there grows a still more dangerous thing: "I have a little food" plus "I have none." If from this problem the sum is "We have a little food," the thing is on its way, the movement has direction... If you who own the things people must have could understand this, you might preserve yourself... But that you cannot know.*

*For the quality of owning freezes you forever into "I," and cuts you off forever from the "we.[14]"*

This is why I do not want to ever have so many possessions that I am tied to them. I do not want to be tied forever into an *I*.

I am wearing an expensive Calvin Klein jacket that my brother bought me. I wish I wasn't.

Downstairs there are about four people having a cell group meeting. They are studying the book of Romans. Sometimes I wonder if the apostle Paul had a bad experience with a woman which makes him judge all of them too harshly.

We are going to take some candles and go back to our cave to pray with some more people. It is a real cave. I will let you know how it goes.

I will be cross with you if you have not at least TRIED leg wrestling yet.

Emily

———◇◇◇———

Dear Aaron,

Quote for the day: God never comes too early or too late, He is always just on time.[15]

My old lady friend Elsie said this to me today because I walked past just as she wants to bend down to pick up some dandelion leaves for her bird. Old people are full of practical wisdom.

Simon and I had an I am not backing down contest. I say *I am not scared of you* and he says *I am not scared of you either*, and we have a staring contest. He puts a piece of popcorn up my nose and I still do not move. To continue with the nose theme – in church today I put something blue on the end of my nose to see if anyone says anything. I have some serious conversations – but no one does. Maybe they have become immune to me, or maybe it is just proof that they never really saw me in first place.

Bible study with our new youth leader was beyond boring. I cannot cope. I let my frustrations show even when I try to hold them in. I am starting to think that if I cannot bring any good out of the situation then I may as well quit and go to another church. Pray for me, I am dropping tears on the computer. I do not believe that we should put a face on to say that everything is OK just because we are Christians.

I should be happy; such a good bike ride with Isabel. I wonder if I am taking too many risks. I decide I'm not because I never fall off – then I do. I always scar my knee in the same place. When I am an old lady, I will look at my knees and smile at the memories. To finish the ride, we sit on a hill drinking hot chocolate and reading Psalms. We can see for miles. These bike rides stop me going mad with the falseness of human existence.

Thank you for listening – I feel better already.

It is good to be seen. I see you even if you won't send a photo.

Emily

Aaron!

Here is a proverb from the Tabloid Bible for you. Sorry.

*Like a sinking ship is man*
*Like a ship that goes down to the depths of the sea*
*For we all have holes in our bottoms*[16]

I am mad today. Mad because it is blue, and I had to sit in church. I was late arriving because I had a worship session of my own. I listened to a CD and looked at the tree outside my house which is bursting with big white blossoms and birds. The environment is sometimes so unnatural in church that God feels less real. It feels like we are floating away from all that is beautiful about the world on a ship that's slowly sinking, and I am the only one who sees it.

The sermon is on forgiveness and there is an alter call. I go forward to forgive the church for making me feel trapped.

I have my art exam in a week and have forgotten how to draw.

I think that it is dangerous of you to say that things that can be explained by science are not spiritual.

Downstairs smells like fish because the fish man has just dropped in for a cup of coffee and he is sitting watching my dad prancing around the sitting room doing a double-handed broadsword demonstration for Dave. Dave has just become a Christian and I can see by his face that he is confused by the whole experience.

In America do Christian youth groups do this thing where they sit in a circle and pass a cup-cake around? I think it is supposed to be a form of Christian sex education. A snotty-nosed kid takes a bite, another drops it by accident, it moves around the circle from grubby hand to grubby hand. When it returns to the youth leader, they hold it up and say, "Who wants to eat this now?" No one ever does. Who would? It is supposed to teach us to save ourselves sexually for when we are married. But I have so many questions I never dare ask! Like what if the cake sits around for so long before being eaten that it becomes stale? And – I hardly dare say this out loud – is there a third way? What would happen if each person who handles the cake does so respectfully? The first adds some icing – the second some sugar sprinkles – the third a cherry – the fourth a candle. You get the idea. Frosting. A dusting of icing sugar. It could become a really great cake. Sexual "sin" seems to happen whether we try to stop it or not. Would it be better to teach respect – rather than guilt and shame? I would not dream of saying these things to anyone. I cannot even say the word *sex* out loud without going bright red, so asking these questions is not an option. What do I know anyway? I guess these adults must know more than me somehow. You won't tell on me, will you?

I have the choice on Friday of either going down to church and doing a display with crepe paper and pompoms for the window, or of going to a cell group at St. Chad's where I can talk about interesting aspects of the Bible with adults who do not seem to have noticed that I am younger than them.

Hope I don't regret sharing so many thoughts with you.

Emily

————◇◇◇————

Aaron,

> *I sometimes dream of giving up all I have and becoming a hospital nurse. I close my eyes and think and dream, and at those moments I feel full of indominatable strength. No wounds, no festering sores could frighten me then... Yes, but how long do you think I could endure such a life?*[17]

I am being too lazy today. Need to recover from the chaos. The house had three little girls in it all morning. My Mum collects them. I go into her bedroom to see what is happening and she is hiding behind her dressing gown (which is hanging on her door). Rest and comfort by themselves are horrible, as they have nothing to contrast with. Contentment is such a risk, because it is the death of striving. The quote is from The Brothers Karamazov. The chapter *A Lady of Little Faith* where the woman talks about active love.

I guess that is also my question. I think that my ideas might be nobler than my actions. Was it C.S. Lewis who said, "The more I love humanity in general, the less I love men in particular[18]"? Dreams and reality are hard to roll into one are they not? Romantic love calls for an immediate act of heroism, but active love means hard work and tenacity. Read that chapter. It is a good book.

But I do not actually understand what you Americans *do* without tea to drink. Tea is more something to be busy with than a drink. I do not like Coca-Cola. It is too sweet. I prefer bitter things. Have you ever tried Guinness or eaten a dandelion leaf?

On Friday night Liz, Isabel and I attempt to go to a youth meeting, but it is cancelled. So, we drive past churches looking for other meetings. We find a dance class and are chased by an old lady who wants us to join in. We think they may have been Mormons. We find another church, but it is empty. There is a sign on the door that says that they only want three pints of milk on a Friday. We leave them an extra one just to be annoying; Liz always carries pints of milk. After this we visit the Simon who used to be a punk before becoming a Christian. He is having a complicated argument about knickers. Rebecca is wearing Lydia's knickers and she is upset because they are her favourites. They are his daughters and are seven and nine.

David Hamilton was the guest speaker last night. He is in the Ulster Volunteer Force before he found God. I can see the parallels between being a Christian and a terrorist. Both feel like ways to use big ideologies to avoid the hard work of active love.

Yes. I agree with you. I think people start the *once saved always saved* questioning when they want to figure out how little they have to do in order to squeeze into Heaven. It is something we will have to talk more about.

Our new youth leader took me aside to tell me that anyone not going to her Tuesday Bible-study is not allowed any ministry in the church. It feels like gaslighting. Can it be called that if I am aware it is happening? I am increasingly confused by the whole situation. Banning people from serving God in their own way is like forcing them to be eternal babies so you can continue to bottle feed them. Maybe I am just fighting for power just like she is?

*How long can we endure such a life?*

Emily

———◇◇◇———

Aaron Dear,

*Imagine a set of people all living in the same building. Half of them think it's a hotel, the other half think it's a prison. Those who think it's a hotel might regard it as being quite intolerable, and those who thought it was a prison might decide that it was really surprisingly comfortable. So that what seems the ugly doctrine is one that comforts and strengthens you in the end. The people who try to hold an optimistic view of the world would become pessimists; the people who hold a pretty stern view of it become optimistic[19].*

It is weird that you read somewhere that it is better to be a pessimist. I read this yesterday. It is from "God in the Dock" by C.S. Lewis.

I am in a good mood. I tell my Royal Rangers (it is like Christian Scouts, do you have it?) that we are going downstairs to do a load of boring work and then sneak all fifteen of them out of the fire-door, so the other group won't find out. Lewis is right: they enjoy themselves more when their expectations are confounded. We go to the river and I blow up balloons for them to burst with stones. A football sails off and I chase it downstream and get wet trousers. Some of the kids are in school uniform and get muddy. I avoid their mothers afterwards.

I meant the Providence/Intervention question. In a way it is related to our Evolution/Creationism debate. Look up the meaning of the words and read the book of Esther. I don't want to explain because I don't want to influence your answer. I am glad that you are not against the idea of God being in control of chance. Does the fact that the Bible says that a strong east wind is blowing mean that it is not him who parts the Red Sea? Creation does not need to have "God did this" written on it in large neon letters. Yes. Science should not cross into religious territory, and religion should not try to dictate science. Wrong. Birds are not created in that order. The original is *winged creatures* (which could mean insects) so the biblical and evolutionary accounts match. It worries me that you say *If evolution is true, then the bible is wrong*. It worries me a lot. Even if that statement causes you no pain, it might cause pain to others.

Are Backpack Sandwiches intentional or accidental? I have eaten accidental ones.

It is funny how people seem to change as you get to know them. I bet I am not who people think I am. You see the inside and they see mostly the outside. Paul Wren (my long-haired friend who rides a bicycle and teaches maths) says that people should stare into each other's eyes for a whole minute before beginning a conversation. Do you think that would be practical?

I can see into the neighbour's garden from here. They are quite new neighbours and Mum has made friends with them. Their garden starts at the end of ours and there is a fence separating them. When they were building it, they left a gap, so mum can go through and have cups of tea. Every now and then when I am writing to you, I see her walk down the garden and disappear.

The Bible is quoted to say that we should submit to authority as it is placed there by God. What about the leaders who place themselves? Should we follow people who are leaders by label only? I think that if Christians are *in God's river* that they will have the hardest parts of themselves worn smooth. This hierarchy (that they love so much) only works in a spirit of humility. If you submit to leaders who are not submitting to God, then you are not submitting to God either. This is my reason for acting like a maverick sometimes. I don't say these things too often because I know I have got a pretty large plank in my own eye. Though I would rather be open about my feelings and risk disproval. If I am wrong people can tell me, I am willing to listen. Did you know that the word *Shalom* does not denote a peace that is devoid of conflict? It means we can be in a beautiful space together despite our differences.

Someone once prophesied that I am going to *break structures in the church*. I tell this to Tim (who is older and wiser than me) once and he says: *You are going to be a lonely bear with a sore head.* I did not know how true this was going to become. I have got nothing against tradition, in fact I think it can be quite beautiful, I just do not like it when it stands in the way of people.

I hope you understand that all this morose talk is the foundation to my possible future happiness.

Yay to pessimism.

Emily

———◇◇◇———

Hey Aaron,

*I have examined so closely my interior and outward life. What strong and strange new gems of hope were born in my soul during those memorable hours! I weighed and decided all sorts of issues — Dostoyevsky*[20]

Last night I go beyond where the street lights end and sit at the top of the hill. I do this sometimes. This is a line from a song: *can we hang out tonight underneath your ceiling, stare up at a million lights and listen to you breathing.* Looking at New Mills when it is spread out beneath me makes my problems seem far away. I feel someone watching. Am I watching the universe? or is the universe watching itself through my eyes?

I have become aware of a great irony. The ideal of a *day of rest* is a biblical one, and Christians are the only ones who do not benefit from it. No wonder they are always stressed out. I did not feel like going to church when I woke up. Dark theories were buzzing around my brain. It is hard to go with the right attitude. The Pastor preached yet another sermon on the theme of revival. Near the end of it he said that there is a gap between the youth group and the rest of the church, which he went on to bridge by putting us down in public. He said things like, "I don't mean to criticize, but..." There is a huge event in Manchester that we are involved in called The Message 2000. and he said that it will never all come together because Jesus isn't the centre. Then he got the worship band to sing *We're coming back to the heart of worship*[21]. The irony is that the song is written by one of the people running the event.

I knew that I would boil if I did not talk to him afterwards. When I spoke to him in his office, he said, "I have seen youth events before and nothing good has ever come of them." He also said that, "If we were actually focused on Jesus, then we would bring our friends to his church rather than to events which are only superficial." He is quite the elitist.

The Pastor's wife calls a meeting to try to act as a mediator between the new youth leader and some of the youth group. I squeeze Liz's arm, thinking *relax, stay calm, talk slowly and quietly.* She tells us that God "always defends his order." I can see things from their side, and it is annoying to be able to see us how they see us: people who make problems from things that exist only in our minds. If these things exist in so many minds, surely they have some reality to them. I think that problems like mine are happening in churches everywhere. New wineskins for new wine and all that. At one point I break and say that I feel like I am being spoon fed. They tell me that I need to change my pace to match the rest of the group. Then Katherine says that she feels like she is being spoon fed too – and they don't say anything.

Maybe I examine things too closely. Maybe I should walk back up that dark hill and see everything from the distance again.

May your perspective be amplified under the reality of the stars.

Emily

Hello Dear Aaron,

*I wake last night, slipping from one reality into a greater one. Dream logic so solid dissolved. Strange how metaphors give insight into living, like life itself sometimes gives insight of another plane just beyond waking. Will looking back from this distant place make the logic of this world seem further removed than a dream from waking? I have this dream in which I know I am dreaming. Frustration mounts as I try to relate this to the characters living there. All too few are these moments of awareness. More often now, I sense these bubbles – wormholes to an overlapping reality. I try to catch one, but the process of study destroys it, the thin image never burning deep enough for retention. I therefore cannot relate these experiences to others, or make them see, for they can only be known first hand. The dismay of not being able to hold them individually for study in the palm of my hand is relieved by the knowledge that these truths are not rare, but hiding in every day. They cannot be contained, but the sweet residue of each builds up a treasured memory.*

I write this after having a strange dream. I woke at five and caught it while it is still alive. I was choosing tea-bags at the bottom of the ocean. Round ones are symbolic of the outside world, round like the sun above you, round like the earth. Square ones represented the indoors; you look up and see only the ceiling. It seemed to make so much sense, but the logic is forgotten now. Do they turn the whole ocean into a giant cup of tea I wonder? Sometimes a cup of tea is the only thing that stops me for long enough to connect me back to the watery oneness of everything.

Today is good. Someone must be praying for me. It is snowing outside, and my heart feels warm. I am not mad at the church. The church is you and my friends, church is conversations that strengthen my heart, church is people who carry the pain and joy of Jesus in their eyes, church is the natural and unforced desire to be one (but never the same).

I heard someone give this message from God recently:

*You have compared one against the other, jockeying for position. Your equality is false. I build differences into my economy because my character is full of differences. How can the differences in me be expressed if you are all trying to be the same?*

I enjoy your stories, Aaron. I don't like waste and greed either. Better to steal for a reason than to vandalise for a kick.

It seems the only way for me to fit into my church's mould is by being something I am not. It is not a problem for those who do fit nicely into the mould. Many people who don't fit have left already – many of them still scarred from the experience of being misinterpreted and apparently rejected. Some people can fit in this space, but it compresses me. I feel I need to break free from the whole construct, like in the Truman Show. Church to me is not the back of someone's head; it is the understanding between hearts. I try to talk like this to our youth leader sometimes, but her face goes blank and I know there will never be understanding between us.

You are right. When you are a kid everything is so special and interesting. Teenagers act like everything is so not cool. Teenagers grow into adults who have little respect or awe for the special things in life. I went through the phase of feigning disinterest, but now God is making me into a child again, and the magic is back in life. Do you think that is what it means to be born again?

I wish I could spend my whole life talking to you, but sleep is a reality I need to escape to from time to time.

May you close your eyes and awake to the faint sounds of watery oneness.

Emily

Hey!

*Stuff your eyes with wonder, he said, live as if you'd drop dead in ten seconds. See the world. It's more fantastic than any dream made or paid for in factories.*[22]

I would like to know how much you want to have adventures. I want to get to the end of life having really lived and experienced it to the absolute full. I want to bite deep into living and not just nibble on the surface. I want to be a shark not a goldfish.

I finished Fahrenheit 451 today. Did you finish yet? I read it sitting in the heather, looking out over Manchester. The view of the city fading out into the haze made the book seem real. I think I might have cried – but I only had ten minutes to ride my bike home in time to help with Royal Rangers. I think the emotion that could have come out in tears came out in energy and speed – which was a good alternative outlet.

Yes. I have lots of thoughts on how *Christian* Christian music should be. I like to think about how Jesus got his message across using parables: *You shall hear, but not understand.* Some people see parables as pointless, because they don't get the message across clearly enough. I love them because they make you think. The only way for anything to become meaningful to you, is if you have discovered it yourself. Curiosity is vital. Is singing about loving each other less *Christian* than singing about loving God? Surely a Christianity that does not connect with the world around it is useless. You cannot fake it though. You cannot *sing about something that is relevant to your audience, so they will like you, and you can save them for Jesus.* That is offensive as well as dumb. Who are we to decide if something is Christian or not; we should just let people be themselves.

Did I tell you what happened in that Christian camp last year? We were studying the beatitudes. I like the one that says: *you are blessed when you are at the end of your rope,* because that was how I felt. It was the end of summer and I could not face another school year without a shift of some sort. It came to the last meeting of the camp and I was desperate. I pray so hard for God to send someone to pray with me. Someone did, but half-heartedly, and I felt sick. The meeting ends and so do my hopes.

Me and Isabel and Liz wander the evacuating site late that night, most people have already left. I get this panicked feeling at the end of festivals; I cannot explain it. It felt like we were picking our way through an eerie battlefield weeks after the battle. After a while we noticed a group of three or four shaking women in the middle of a path. The shaking slows eventually, and I asked them what was happening. One of the women (she is French) told me that they didn't know what was going on either, but that God was doing something interesting. They offered to pray for us and did so until 3 a.m. I went to get sleeping bags and we huddled in them, eating rice cakes, still in the middle of the path. The security guards did not know what to make of it. There were visions of rabbits released from hutches, hundreds and thousands raining down on me like the skittles advert, and of black and white photos changing to colour. I was on a high for days after. Months after. Now. I am glad for that experience; it gave me the strength I needed to keep going.

I hope that you too can draw the strength you need from some beautiful and unusual places.

That you stuff your eyes with wonder, as if you'd drop dead in ten seconds.

But that you don't drop dead because I need someone to talk to.

Emily

Dear Friend,

I have the short-lived feeling that you get after doing something that has been looming, like a geography essay.

I don't know what the outcome is going to be with the church situation. I might *talk to Brenda*. *Talking to Brenda* has sort of become a catch-phrase in our church. If you have problems, you *talk to Brenda* or *get Brenda to pray for you*. She has this way of looking at you which means you cannot lie when she asks you how you are. It is disconcerting. Sometimes she draws things out that you wish she hadn't, but you cannot look away. It is like being mesmerised by a magician with a scarf of knotted handkerchiefs, coming out of your guts and not her sleeve.

I read your long email in church; hid it in my bible during the sermon. Almost as naughty as pretending to pray when you are actually sleeping (Elsie!).

Like you, I have also made a pact not to become more boring as I get older. As a kid I wrote a letter to my future children asking them to hold me accountable to that. I think I will always prefer climbing trees to sitting in restaurants. You know I still do not know what your face looks like. Do you think we will ever meet? Would it change everything? Would we just talk in really short sentences, and shrug in answer to each other's questions?

It is now definite that I am going to Argentina in September. I think I am going to miss our regular correspondence more than I miss anything else.

Thank you for being in my life Aaron,

Emily

Dear Aaron,

*I have no solutions for intellectual problems, but I have a solution for humanity: love.* [23]

— Reading The Brothers Karamazov changed me.

I flicked the TV on last night and watched a debate about the Kansas *evolution problem*. There before me stands your hero Ken Ham, sandwiched between an evolutionist who believes in God, and one who does not. I like Ken Ham the least, his eyes are dead, and he is dogmatic. I would never have guessed that he is a Christian. He has no respect for the others or the arguments they are making. I think that the spirit behind an argument is sometimes more important than the argument itself. Sometimes I listen to a sermon and something imparts to me, even though I understand little of what was said. *It is the person who speaks, not the words.* Other times I can listen to a brilliantly composed sermon and leave unaffected because the speaker has no life in them. I met an American who reminded me of Ken Ham a few years ago. His sermon seems to make sense, but he was dead behind the eyes, and what he says when he prays for me is downright weird.

OK, you said, and I quote: *Darwin wanted an explanation for the world that did not include God.* This is not true. He speaks of creation as having been *breathed by the Creator.* That is a quote from Origin of the Species. I just read it. I have also been wondering about where you think Cain's wife came from. Bible makes it sound like there are cities already there when Cain leaves Adam and Eve. It is a bit icky if the only answer you have is incest. Must have been a lot of incest if cities formed so quickly.

How are the cool people? It is probably just a mask. I find it hard to get the right balance between loving like I have never been hurt and not throwing pearls before swine. I think it is best to veer towards keeping your heart open.

I must go and paint some trees before the blue fades.

Literally cannot wait to hear about the socks.

E.

Hi Aaron,

Just got back from Royal Rangers. By some miracle (that cannot be explained by science) I managed to keep them occupied without incident.

I cannot for the life of me understand why your thinking is so oppositional regarding science and Genesis. Don't you understand that circles and squares can be shadows of the same object? Don't worry about it too much: I think I am in a place that you do not believe exists. I hate that you think I compromise the truth. The truth is a songbird that I can hear sing from time to time. If you cage it, it will never sing the song it did when it was free.

You think that evolution inspired Hitler? If a man killed his wife with a rolling pin would you ban rolling pins? What about how Romans 13 allowed the German church to turn a blind eye? *All governments have been placed in power by God.* Should we ban the Bible in case it is misused?

Another question: If animals do not have a spirit or consciousness, why does my cat have such a definite *I am* look to him?

I just had a good conversation with my five-year-old friend, Larry. He said he would rather stay in preschool and not go to school. He said he doesn't like it when they make him think, then tell him off for thinking wrong. He has a good point.

We have new neighbours moving in. Mum made them a cake. I should imagine they will be better than the old neighbour. She thumped Father Christmas when he visited because his sleigh was too noisy.

I wish I could be more like your bus driver and leave the future to fight its own battles. My future haunts my present. I am the same person then that I am now, the future me inhabits the present me. It is hard to explain, but it is like there is a bit of me in all of humanity, and a bit of me in all of time. As much as I believe in living in the moment, I cannot believe that the moment is all there is. As I am writing this I am looking back at myself from the future. Do you do that?

*All*. This is *all* for today. As my CD sings its final song, and my eyes filter in the last light of the day, and my brain and the computer start to shut down until a new day reboots them again. I will forget tomorrow and will rest in the death of today, and in dreams, and in Heaven, and in sleep.

Emily

Dear Aaron,

*Except for the point, the still point, there would be no dance, and there is only the dance. —TS Eliot*[24]

I am taking the widest view of life. I am looking up from that one quietly spinning point into the vastness of the universe. Once God starts to flood all of everything, you start to sense Him in the details. I am starting to realise that all you can do is what is at hand to be done. I am thinking that my mind is a good place to start. Everything is conceived in the mind and without it there is no birth. Maybe even your unvoiced prayers change the world before leaving your mind.

I have added *deep contemplation* to my list of pastimes. I guess the phase I am going through is also something to do with my age. With my whole life ahead of me I need to decide who I am, what I believe in, and where I am going. I have decided that there is too much of God for me to know all of Him, but I have to start somewhere. I do not want to waste time on things that are unimportant.

All we can do is to be devoted to the truth we think we have. Isn't that right Aaron?

Emily

P.S. When I got home from a youth meeting in a neighbouring town, I found a tiny handwritten poem rolled inside a drinking straw at the bottom of my bag.

*Into this world comes a maiden,*
*a darkly raven-haired beauty,*
*whose hidden female mysteries swirl in deep dark pools*
*on occasion to be glimpsed at by the gifted observer*
*behind the windows of her soul.*
*Born in the heart of God, a pure heart,*
*kind and tender, is superficially covered by a*
*youthful zeal and restless excitement.*
*How blessed the man who is invited*
*past those portals to rest his head*
*on the inner sanctum of her skilled heart;*
*where lie her deeper truths.*
*Who knows where will blow this lively spirit?*
*Where the Spirit leads.*
*Who knows where will rest the deeper soul?*

*Where the Spirit grants her acceptance, love and peace,*
*truly given from a pure and sincere heart*
*seeking no reward save that of being received.*
*She will be given and shared amongst those*
*for whom she has been sent,*
*each adding to the completion of her whole,*
*one day to be gathered and returned, fulfilled,*
*to the very centre of His heart,*
*there to rest and rejoice in love and warmth,*
*forever.*

I am not sure where it came from or what to make of it.

That question has been just one of many plaguing me today.

Aaron!

*In truth, the essence of human life exists in every present time, and*
*therefore requires only depth of comprehension in order to be ex-*
*haustively known.*[25]

I bought a copy of Anna Karenina for £1. This is from the intro. I feel
that it explains everything that my life is about. This is exactly what I
discovered when I went hiking with my friends. We were on top of a hill
and could see for miles and I suddenly felt connected to everything. I
knew that travelling to see the Taj Mahal would not help me feel more
connected. I knew that nothing I did or saw would get me any closer to
what I already felt part of. I asked my friends if they would be happy if
they died in that moment, and they said no; they had not had enough
experiences. Experiences are overrated because the whole of existence is condensed into any one moment. It is possible to travel to the

ends of the earth and to find that the thing you were looking for was inside you all along.

I experienced my own personal sunrise this morning. The only other human awake was the milkman; I assumed he was too busy to appreciate the sky. Mine. All mine! Ground mist dispersed as shards of light tore through thin curtains of cloud. When the display was over, I found a dewy meadow and fell asleep in the long grass for half an hour. I like to pretend that I am as small as a bug. I love God for creating such comical things as bugs. Every day should begin from this tiny perspective.

Do you think it is strange the way your head drains overnight and gradually refills during the next day? That is what my head is doing now. It is like a slow liquid sunrise.

Have you told your parents about me yet?

Emily

A,

Argentina is fast approaching, and I am glad. I want real life! I have been so fed up of being cooped up in middle class comfort when I know that the world that I am out of touch with is a mess. Does that irritate you too? Like I am sitting with my eyes closed and the mess is still there. A lot of people can pretend it isn't, but I can feel it exists. I have always known that I want to be in places where I can make a difference. I do not know yet if those places will be more painful than the boredom I have faced up until now...

There is a baby in my church who is dying from cancer and some people are telling the mother, "Won't it be great when God heals her?" I think this kind of talk can be damaging. I want to hug her and say nothing. But I am not old enough for that to mean anything.

I just realised something sad. I gave up on my church situation. As a youth group we had something going, but I got tired of fighting the church at large and gave up. As a result, I have become accustomed to it just being me and God. It is going to be a challenge for me to open up my faith to others at YWAM. I want someone with skin on today. I feel that you are the closest I have got to church. I *meet* with you more than I meet with people in meetings.

You have reached that age haven't you. If you want to rebel, then there are two ways to do it:

1. Breakaway from the church and become like the rest of the world, which is just another form of conformity.

2. Rebel by radically becoming who you are and who you want to be. It is the hardest option but the healthiest and most rewarding in the long run.

I know you Aaron. I know you will make the right choice. I know you will spread your great big beautiful wings and fly like I am about to when the time is exactly right. My time with you has been more important to me than you could ever imagine. You are my favourite person in all the world. I want you to know that I see you. Even though I barely know what you look like. Even though we don't agree on a lot of things. Living with my parents can be difficult, so the chance to hide away and write you these long emails has been a way to make my life beautifully bearable.

Don't forget to send me your address so I can write you letters.

E.

CHAPTER 3

# Discipleship Training School

When I told my mother that I was going to Argentina with a Christian organisation called Youth With a Mission she was dismissive and said that if God wants me to go, then *He* would have to provide the money. A few days later she comes home late after an evening meeting and calls upstairs to where I am sleeping.

"Emily! What do you call this? Come here!"

As I stumble out of bed, she thrusts a canvas sack in my face. It has my name scrawled on the outside in biro, and inside is £2,500 cash.

"Well..." I say, "I guess this means God wants me to go to Argentina."

I never find out who pushed that bag through the church's letterbox, but it is enough money to get me to Argentina, and enough to make my mother think that to argue with me about it would mean arguing with God.

YWAM (pronounced *why-wham*) is top of the list when it came to Christian Gap Years. I am going to be part of something called Year for God, a year-long program which gives me the choice of three countries: Russia, Uganda, or Argentina. I don't know much about any of these countries, but Argentina sounds the most exciting. The best thing is that my friend Isabel agrees, and decides to come with me.

This is by far the biggest thing we have ever done. I don't think that either of us has ever been away from home for longer than two weeks. But we are not complete strangers to challenge; we had cycled across the country together only a few months previously. It took us three days and only the occasional map reading-mishap to get from one coast to the other. The other cyclists we encountered en route were far better equipped and had been training hard. We decided to do it on a whim the day before. These endurance skills might have been related to our pastimes growing up. New Mills was not exactly a cultural melting pot – we created our own entertainment. On numerous occasions we were driven blindfolded deep into the countryside and left to find our own way home. We quickly learnt to have a good sense of direction. Isabel had even broken the record amongst the church kids by climbing a pillar and staying up there for over half an hour. Surely a year in Argentina would not be too much for us.

I have ten notebooks from my four years in Argentina spread out before me. All of them jammed with short reflections, verses from the Bible, prophecies scrawled on the backs of receipts, diary entries written during enforced *quiet times* with God, and fragments of correspondence to and from the UK. I know that it is not going to be an easy pile to sift through. The content of these four years will probably always be something that I will struggle to understand. The YWAM bubble that I live in always makes complete sense from the inside, but there is a lot of distortion when looking back in from the outside. Or is it the other way around?

The writings that I am flicking through are the frantic pickings of a magpie – someone desperate to store away shiny fragments of meaning. I go to Argentina to search for evidence of something bigger than myself. But, like a magpie, I am mostly scratching at things that have fallen to the ground. What I do not realise until a long time afterwards is that I have had what I am looking for since the very beginning. Living close to the sea and the mountains in North Wales as a young child is the closest I have been to existing alongside the mysteries of God. The deep longing I have to return to that place is not geographical: it is spiritual. I am not talking about the need to see God reflected in nature – I am talking about the need to face the greatness of nature from the untainted perspective of a young child, free from the constructs of adulthood. My time in Wales is a time before I apply labels to things, a time before I learn to say long words, a time before I learn to see the world through a distorted lens. It is a time when I just see. It is a time when I just know. Walls are built the second I learn to say the word *God*. Ironically, the time before my conversion is the closest I am to knowing these mysteries. I don't know this when I step off the plane in Buenos Aires. It will be a long time before I start to.

## Wild Swimming

*When I see water as a child, I remove my clothes and run towards it*
*Wanting to be swallowed into the liquid gut of its otherness*
*Wanting my toes to reach the point that they can't quite touch*
*Wanting the hardness of the earth to sink beneath me*
*Wanting to push the ground away and spin*
*Like I can on a rope swing.*

*When I see water as an adult, I want to remove*
*all I know and run towards it*
*Wanting to embrace the water-born child who is left here*
*Wanting to return to the point before I learn to speak*
*Wanting the hardness of words to sink like stones*
*Wanting to push them away and spin*
*Like the Earth did when she was young.*

## 15ᵗʰ September 2000

First thing that hits when we touch down in Buenos Aires is a crisp wave of cool air that washes over me as we disembark. It is an atmosphere you can inhale deeply: like breathing for the first time. You can read books or watch videos, but you don't know what a place truly feels like until it is inside you. Second thing I notice are all the gay taxi drivers. Cabs line up outside the airport, clustered around them are men of all shapes and sizes touching and hugging each other. Talking so close that they could use the reflections in each other's eyes to straighten their moustaches. Third thing I notice, as we start to drive towards the YWAM Base, are the cars: jalopies that make me feel like I am watching an old American movie, driven in a way that explains the dents and missing parts. Houses lining the highway are pieced together in a similar fashion. The fourth thing is the dogs. Dogs everywhere. A dog sitting alone in the dust pretending to scratch a flea. More dogs on the street than trash cans. A whole gang of dogs sitting around like bored extras in a low budget Spanish language version of a canine Disney movie. Nowhere you can look without seeing a dog. Like Lady and the Tramp, but devoid of romance.

I like the YWAM base. Big wall around it and that contains a collection of little white houses as well as a massive half-built building where we will sleep and have our meetings. There is a pool! Steve (a leader from England who looks like he might have a sense of humour) tries to scare us with stories of what these next two weeks will be like. To aid our transition, we will each be staying with a different local family for the first two weeks. He passes around Yerba Mate (a smoky herb drunk through a shared metal straw from a gourd) so that we can get the face pulling out of the way before our families make us drink it. He then gives us something sweet called *dulce de leche* on crackers and refers to it as *merienda*, which is the meal they have between lunch and dinner. I always thought of adding extra hours to the day, but never considered adding extra meals. All good so far.

## 16th September 2000

House and the family I am staying with are both pleasant. Feel welcome and comfortable. Dusty streets canopied by large waxy leaved trees and tiled floors are cool underfoot. Late nights here, managed to sleep in until twelve. Rebecca takes me to a church in a rough area, watch her teach a dance to a large group of kids. Amazing number of boys taking part enthusiastically. Stay for the service. Her dad is the Pastor. Rebecca apologises for it being boring, but nothing is boring because it is new. Feel more comfortable here than in the churches back home. I like the concrete floor and the sunlight you can see through the gaps in the cracked walls. A man is playing a song on a guitar and I am just thinking how unemotional he looks when he suddenly stops and bursts into tears. It is a country where boys dance and men cry.

## 17<sup>th</sup> September 2000

Bad day. Large collection of toilet stories. Expecting toilet stories, but not so soon. Nearly break the toilet. Don't want to talk about it. Spend all morning being sick, so they give me a charcoal pill to settle my stomach. Still sick all afternoon, but now the sick is black. Bit better by the evening. The problem is adapting to the food too fast. Mum taught me to eat what is given me and I can do that. Stomach is not too keen on the idea, especially because I swallow things without chewing (I hate olives!). Meal times are not easy. Read some good verses from the Bible about the value of suffering.

## 18<sup>th</sup> September 2000

Relaxing day so far. Huge piece of beef for lunch. Drink Yerba Mate in the park: starting to get used to it. Watching 'The Simpsons' in Spanish. Voices sound wrong; it is like being in a parallel universe. Soap opera that was on earlier makes some of the British versions look highly intellectual. Storm last night and the thunder wakes me. Feel suddenly scared at the prospect of being here for a whole year. Have the feeling I get when I jump off something high into an expanse of water. Mid-air and wishing I wasn't. Trying to remember that the feeling only lasts a moment before inevitable joy or oblivion.

## 20ᵗʰ September 2000

Rebecca lives with her parents, her sister, and her sister's family. They share one house because of Argentina's economic situation. Her dad works hard, but his work is unstable. Something to do with aluminium. Her parents smile at me a lot and keep checking that I am *bien* and that I am wearing socks.

Meet up with some of the others who will be doing the Discipleship Training School. They all seem very interesting. Makes me feel boring and inferior. Need to take the subway home by myself. Lisa from Colombia prays that God will send people to help me. Meet a very well-dressed old lady called Peggy who takes me nearly all the way home. Her mother was British, so she speaks with an old-fashioned English accent. Think I must be the tallest person in the whole of South America, my height is the first thing that people comment on, "You're tall," they say, as if giving me new information. At least having dark hair helps me blend in a little.

## 25ᵗʰ September 2000

Cake again for breakfast: I am getting fat. Now I am eating *merienda*. I always think it is dinner and eat way too much. Biggest ant I have ever seen is sitting right next to me, I have given him a crumb and he thinks it is Christmas. Rebecca and I have reached the awkward silence phase, which is not surprising seeing as we've spent two weeks together. Grateful for this time with her family, but ready to see what challenges my time with YWAM is going to bring.

Before continuing, I would like to explain a little about the history and formation of YWAM.

Youth With A Mission was founded by Loren Cunningham and his wife Darlene in 1960. Loren was the son of Assemblies of God pastors, who received his own missionary call at the age of thirteen. During a missions trip to the Bahamas in 1956, Loren had a vision of waves lapping the shorelines of the world's continents, the waves grew in strength until they covered the world. Looking more closely, he saw that the waves were made up of an army of young people, spreading the word of God. Today, YWAM has an estimated 20,000 full-time workers in 171 countries. The introductory phase is formed around a Discipleship Training School: A full-time program that lasts five or six months, consisting of two parts: a lecture phase (know God) and an outreach phase (make Him known).

I have no diary entries for a while now. Just an endless torrent of notes taken during the three-month lecture phase of my Discipleship Training School (DTS). The subjects covered include:

- CLEAN CONSCIENCE (How to defeat the power of sin in our lives)
- WHAT KIND OF A GENERATION DO WE WANT TO BE? (Are we going to be survivors like Lot, or dreamers like Abraham)
- VALUES OF YWAM (Visionaries, International and Interdenominational, Extended structure, Relationship, Individuals, Youth, Character before ministry, Generosity)
- REVIVAL (Living out the dreams of God)
- PRIDE (Walking around with masks on)

- THE KINGDOM OF GOD (It is within us and is manifested through the Holy Spirit to the world)
- THE ARTS (Representing a realm that cannot be seen. Art as spiritual warfare)
- SERVICE (To serve each other without seeking reward)
- THE CHARACTER OF GOD (We cannot know God and remain unchanged)
- RENEWING OUR MINDS (Lean not on your own understanding)
- ANCESTRAL BONDAGES (The ties of the past affect my present and lead to my future)
- SPIRITUAL WARFARE (Our struggle is not against flesh and blood, but against powers and principalities)
- THE BRIDE OF CHRIST (The church is Christ's betrothed and He wants her to be beautiful)
- SPIRITUAL AUTHORITY (Submit to God before people)
- FREE MASONRY (Gog and Magog unite with Satan for final battle)
- INNER HEALING (Letting God mend the cracks in our clay jar so he can fill us)
- TIES OF CONTROL (The proud have set a trap to catch us)
- FASTING (Controlling appetite and taming the flesh)
- COMMITMENT (Service to God is for our whole life)
- TRUTH (A bomb that must be wrapped in love and detonated by the Holy Spirit)

- THE DIVINE PLUMBLINE (Swinging between rejection and rebellion, needing to come in line with the truth of God's love)
- FORGIVENESS (Fresh beginnings in Christ)
- MISSIONS (I will bless you and you will be of blessing)
- RELATIONSHIPS (Dating as the world understands it is not Biblical)
- SPIRITUAL POWER OF MONEY (Most talked about subject in the Bible)
- GOALS DREAMS AND VISIONS (Only limitation is my understanding of who God is)
- BROKENNESS (Maturity is found in times of wilderness)

There is fun to be had too. Muddy football matches, where only the whites of our eyes are left clean. The time Laura caught and ate a flying beetle, to prove that of course girls can eat bugs. The time Ramon (the resident handy-man) was mending my bunk and the slats broke under his not unsubstantial weight and he was left on the bottom bunk with his legs still on the top bunk, completely unable to move from laughter. Friendships are forming, beautiful deep friendships. I am quite in love with Anna from Israel, we talk and walk, swinging our arms with our little fingers linked together.

## 24ᵗʰ October 2000

Feel pressurised to have problems. Do not think the leaders believe me when I say I cannot identify any. Maybe they are buried too far down. Maybe the tiny earthquakes on the surface of my life are indicators of bigger faults deep inside. A leader prays for me at small group. Talks about an area in the inner me that I will not open to

God. Uses strong words like "self-hate" and "false strength." Week of Inner-Healing. Need God to reveal what I need to change.

## 28ᵗʰ October 2000

Deliverance Week (I think deliverance is another word for exorcism). Want to write what I remember quick – it is already a bit blurry like how I imagine people feel after taking psychedelics. No one prays for me during the first meeting, become aware of a deep-rooted loneliness. Cannot remember a time when I have not felt it. Scares me. Feel it curled around my heart like a huge black cat, purring soothingly, but wanting to squeeze the love out. Receive prayer in the next meeting. Someone senses a spiritual blockage. Makes me remove my jewellery (bracelets and necklaces can be symbolic of slavery). They find Masonic symbols on one of my bracelets and destroy it. Cannot explain in Spanish that all silver bracelets have hallmarks. If I cannot trust these people to take care of my jewellery, how can I trust them to take care of my soul?

In the evening Juliana from Brazil prophesises over me. Says God has huge plans for my life. Then Rosa ministers. Want to talk about loneliness, but she prays for that without prompting. Prays against a spirit of early death, which is interesting as Juliana has just prophesised that I would live a long life. Feel at peace, even though my body is shaking slightly. At one-point (my eyes are closed) Rosa symbolically unbinds my mind with a hand movement around my head. Translator says that my head moves in a motion that coincides with hers. Rosa asks if I can think of an object that might have spiritual power over me. Instantly remember a monkey I have back home that is carved out of a coconut. *See no evil, hear no evil, speak no evil*. Shows how I feel shut out from the world, isolated and unable to express myself: unable to see, hear or speak. She prays that this shell will be removed from my mind.

As soon as I wake up something feels different. I walk down Martin Fierro (to go to the internet café) feeling lighter: as if the air is more transparent. I feel other emotions more too. Maybe if you block out the hard emotions, you block the good ones also.

## 30th November 2000

Outreach teams change around again. Anna no longer with us. Going to an oil refinery town instead of to a nature reserve. Maybe God wants to break me. The dances we are having to learn are breaking me. There is one where we dress up in bed sheets and pretend to be African whilst waving sticks. It is supposed to be a prophetic act, but I feel stupid.

Last night, as we come back on the bus from the all-you-can-eat restaurant, Anna dozes with her head on my shoulder. Tears roll silently down my cheeks as old lies resound: you have no-one, no-one will understand you now, no-one will ever get close to you, you are alone, the one person able to understand you is going somewhere else and you will never see her again.

Today feels the same. I need someone to fight through it with me; the fact I cannot find anyone makes me feel even more alone. Everyone seems to be having such good quiet times with God; I am starting to compare. I write this diary while everyone else is in direct communication with The Divine. Have a conversation with Nick and he says that I am stranger than him, because even he does not understand me.

## 6th December 2000

Alejandro Gomez anoints us as warriors with Indian war paint. He is a pastor with extremely shiny bucket-cut hair that moves more than he does, which is a lot. I do so want to be a fighter – my mind is such a battleground.

## 22nd December 2000

Given away so many things that I am starting to feel dried up. Samantha has given away so much that she only has one pair of shoes and three T-shirts. I think she is giving obsessively – I am worried for her health. Though I do want to pull and stretch myself out in all directions. Don't care how much it hurts. Tired to the point of exhaustion: like I cannot put one foot in front of the other. Glad to be going to Chile for Christmas. Hope I get to rest.

## 25th December 2000

Woken at six by about ten dogs barking at our tents. Discover the Christmas socks that AnnMarie has strung up for us, stuffed with goodies and soggy bananas. Camping on a YWAM surf school in Pichilemu. Done some surfing, but the waves are big for beginners. 24-hour bus journey over the Andes to get here is breath-taking. Route through like a concertinaed snake, which brings us up close to Mount Aconcagua (the second highest mountain outside the Himalaya). Sometimes I feel like I could learn more from The Mountains than I could from a school. I would have liked to have got off the bus and stayed there for a week by myself.

Christmas dinner was awesome. Go to a restaurant by the sea (one of the dogs follows us and waits outside while we eat). Ask the waiter for a typical dish from the area and he serves me conga eel soup. It is the most delicious thing I have ever eaten.

CHAPTER 4

*Outreach*

## 7ᵗʰ January 2001

Christmas in Chile was needed. Landscape released built-up pressure – so much so that on boxing day I completely collapse, body breaks down like it should have done months before.

Outreach started. Insanely long coach journey and here we are in the windiest oil refinery town in Patagonia: *Comodoro Rivadavia*. Do not know what to expect other than more mental exhaustion. Feel like I am finally where I am meant to be - not really a class-room sort of person. I don't think I've felt like myself for a while.

Church yesterday. Only partially built, not much more than a pile of rubble – I like it. The Pastor's first church was a tiny cara-van which expanded slowly. Congregation is mostly gypsies. One of them wants me to marry her son. The team tease me about it. He is very creepy looking, and I feel very uncomfortable and a little sick.

## 9ᵗʰ January 2001

Served a lovely breakfast by Banana (a gypsy who has lots of sis-ters named after different pieces of fruit). She has long braided hair and a serious face that does not look like it deserves a silly name.

Drive up the coast and spot sea lions and porpoises. Ten of us in a battered blue Ford Falcon that has a suicidal urge to pull to the right near cliffs. At one point the Pastor (still wearing his suit) urges us to climb up a high pier where we race up and down in a little cart on rails, until we are spotted by the authorities. He has not done stuff like this before. I think he loves us. Spiritual joy is moving into everyday life, which is where it should be.

Later we pray at a spot known as Devil's corner, about fifty kids come to talk with us and pray to become Christians with Carlos from Ecuador.

Banana cooked us food again very late in the evening. As we – finally! – leave for bed, Franchesca says, "Hasta mañana hermana Banana," which translates to, "See you tomorrow sister Banana." I think that it is perhaps the best sentence that anyone has ever said – in Spanish or in any language.

## 10th January 2001

We go to pray near a statue of a woman with the whole of Patagonia at her feet which stands on the road near the city limits. There is a day care centre nearby run by a woman who does witchcraft. The children and their parents keep dying in mysterious ways, or so we are told. Spiritual warfare is interesting. It feels like you are standing together to push away a giant heavy invisible cloud. Praying so hard that it feels like you are in an actual physical battle. Or an argument. I have been in arguments and felt my blood boil – it is a little like that. You pray until the argument is resolved, and the cloud evaporates.

This evening I said I would give Carlos $1 to eat a little piece of bread and Marmite – Jeremy always carries some. He upped me to $5 and was sure the money was his. But no! Half went in, his face contorted, and half came out. It was not physically possible for him to swallow it. Not for everyone I suppose.

1:40 a.m. Banana is starting to heat the water for our dinner.

## 13ᵗʰ January 2001

3:20 a.m. Just back from a wedding where we did not know the Bride or the Groom. Carlos went up to the front to preach a long gospel message. Felt awkward for stealing the lime-light and for the fact that we ate such a lot of food. I think that people think that we are God's messengers and that He will bless them if they bless us. I'm not sure what I think about them thinking that.

## 18ᵗʰ January 2001

Insane evening. Put on a puppet show high up on a hill in an *extension* (rough neighbourhood). Krysten proudly announces (on the microphone in Spanish) that "God is the only God in the Whole University." Such a spirit of violence. Fighting. Throwing things. Look in their eyes not exactly playful. Met three kids who have lost their parents and are forced to live with their ancient grandparents. Grandad an alcoholic and grandmother had a fall and cannot care for them, so they take care of themselves. My heart is so broken that it has decided to opt out of things for a while. My mind will have to take over for a bit.

I am the world's worst missionary. Stopped seeing the point of evangelism. Do not see why the world needs more Christians. What changes when someone repeats a prayer just to get us to stop talking to them? Is that really all it takes to get someone into heaven? If they end up going to church how does that help? Would rather just put my arms around them and let them know I care. Making the gospel appear like a quick fix solution for people's problems is not helpful. Truth cannot be pinned down like a bug in a frame. It is a direction to run in, something to chase with a butterfly net (and maybe never catch). Not a second-hand thing. Cannot be inherited or purchased in an expensive Bible with concordance features. We cannot fake possession of it.

We fit twelve people in the car on the way back.

Jeremy and Sarah and I prepared *Cena*. Managed to get Louisa to leave the kitchen – she does too much for an older woman. She met The Pastor when she became a Christian in Mendoza ten years ago. By coincidence she bumped into him down here, shortly after her husband left her for *not being good enough around the house*. She works so hard and it is good to see her sitting down.

## 22<sup>nd</sup> January 2001

Trip to The Petrified Forest in Sarmiento today. Five hours to drive 170km. Everything about the journey is unsafe: ten in the car, no seatbelts, worn tyres, faulty steering, big holes in chassis, long journey through uninhabited land, maniac driver. We do not need health and safety because we have Jesus. Road is nothing but rubble. Pastor driving so fast it sounds like thunder. Pebbles come through the gaps in the floor and sting our legs. Another flat tyre (third of the day!).

Petrified Forest is impressive. Fossilised tree trunks strewn as far as we can see. Easy to imagine dinosaurs smashing them to the ground with their giant tails. Wind so strong that we can lean back into it and let it take our weight, as if supported by the invisible arms of ancient history.

Stop again to get the tyres pumped on the way home. Another on the verge of popping.

Pee publicly three times today. The first is when I am by the highway behind a small hillock; have not realised I am invisible to cars, but not truck drivers. Second is when I am just pulling up my trousers discreetly when Kelo (the Pastor's Labrador puppy of a sidekick) comes bounding towards me before covering his eyes in panic and retreating backwards. Third is when we find a service station and gleefully think we will be able to pee in an actual toilet. They are – of course – out of order. Four of us girls go to the back of the building and pee in a row on the count of three. Realise shortly after that we have been caught on security camera and broadcast in the foyer to people queuing to buy coffee and *galletitas*.

## 24ᵗʰ January

Children's home this morning. Discover how to electrocute the children with the slide. Static means that if you touch them as they are sliding down you get electrocuted. Make a chain of four children who can all get shocked at once.

In an old people's home at the moment. Jeremy and I talk to an old man who says he is a Catholic, but who does not like the Bible because it makes people angry. We are watching the Jesus Film with them. I hate it. I like to imagine that Jesus experienced actual emotion.

Walk home late through an interesting neighbourhood – hear gunshots.

## 25ᵗʰ January 2001

So tired I am practically in tears. Still struggling with knowing how to communicate the gospel. I am not sure I know what the gospel actually is. Again. Bad missionary. Talk to three kids who spend their time on the streets looking for money. Eight-year-old seems to have a drink problem. They watch me perform a drama called *La Carga* (The Burden). It shows my character's journey through life – when bad things happen, or when I sin, more weight gets added to the bag I am carrying – until I meet Jesus and he takes the weight from me. I look at the faces of the kids as I perform, and I think about my own life. I am supposed to have found Jesus and I still feel the weight of it all. And how do you expect kids who live on the streets not to sin? *They have to steal to survive!* Are bad things supposed to stop happening as soon as we meet Jesus? Might there be a way for bad things to happen without us having to carry them like burdens? Might it be possible to make mistakes without the label of *sin* turning them into the guilt that weighs us down so much? Why can't hard life events and mistakes just roll over us and leave us clean like we are in a cold but cleansing shower?

## 26th January 2001

Sarah's 30th. She is a school teacher from London and if she was back home it would have been a day of huge celebrations. Day starts badly because it is Fran's idea to pretend we are fasting so we can surprise her. Sarah is fuming, we share a room and I am not sure what to do. Maybe it is good for her to be forced to surrender her right to have the sort of birthday she wants? Works out OK because The Pastor drives us to *a brother's* house, where there is a feast laid out for her. Beautiful people from the church who are descended directly from Mapuche Indians.

## 27th January 2001

Swim in the sea then fall asleep on the beach. Ears fill up with sand because of the wind. Everyone (and I mean everyone) goes forward to sing a song at the church service. It is like Christian Karaoke. Karaoke is one of my greatest fears. Christian Karaoke doubly so. Don't start cooking the evening meal until 3 a.m. Been very irritable recently. Snap at Sarah when she asks for more leg room in the car. Don't think anyone believes it is because I am tired; going from nine hours to an average of six is a bit of a jump. Fran talks about someone last year who used tiredness as a method of retreat and a way to succumb to a spirit of rejection.

## 30th January 2001

Morning in the church balancing on a plank between two step ladders bashing a window in a wall with a large mallet. Jesus is my safety net – I think.

Have a water fight before the church service. Quickly turns into a full-scale war. Buckets, then a hose, and finally head dunking in a barrel. We are sat in wet clothes for our last meeting there. People give little speeches about how much we blessed them. A woman made us a huge cake. Jeremy looked very sweet dancing with the tambourine. English people do not move their hips like Latin people, especially tall lanky ones from London. Think he will miss the bearded gypsy worship group. I will miss how they argue about musical differences and calm down seconds before the fists come out. Exciting to be meters away from what feels like a drunken brawl whilst sitting in church.

Moving to a more rigid church next month.

Carlos and Flor say they are going to adopt me which is nice.

## 1st February 2001

These weeks are going to be challenging. Sleeping on a hard church floor. Pastor's wife talks a lot about all the bad things the English have done and about how there will be a lot more women than men in Heaven. She thinks that Krysten is a boy – maybe she has never seen a girl with short hair. New Pastor says that he wants a hundred percent production from us.

## 4th February 2001

I am disappointed that the joy and peace I feel after *Deliverance Week* does not seem to have lasted.

The Pastor (the previous one) brought us pastries. He still loves us. Talk about evolution and creationism around the breakfast table. Mention that I like the YWAM teaching, "Do not teach as truth anything that is debateable." Christianity in general would be more appealing if people followed that guideline.

Still frustrated. My desire for a practical rather than a purely theological faith led me away from my home church and to YWAM. Adapt my expectations when I realise that the lecture phase focuses on personal development. Now in this practical part of the DTS the language barrier prevents me from connecting with people and I am carried along with the current, giving out evangelism tracts that promote a gospel that I am not sure makes sense. Wonder if this constant longing for a more authentic outpouring of faith will ever go away.

Cry last night when Sarah and Fran tell me they love me. They are like, "we cannot believe how messy she is – but we love her." When I wake up, I notice that they have hung my walking sandals outside the window because they smell bad. Maybe they don't love all of me.

## 9th February 2001

*Our* Pastor comes back to take us off for an adventure. A sigh of *here we go again* ripples around the group. At 10 pm we all climb into the back of a pick-up. After an hour's drive down gravelled roads, we arrive at a campsite in the middle of nowhere. Dozens of people with tents and a smouldering campfire, all lit by a single lightbulb. I preach about relying on God's strength and not on our own, and I don't know why – but I don't get scared anymore. Maybe it is because my heart broke from exhaustion and has not mended enough to be able to communicate fear. Three seconds before starting, the electricity cuts and the lightbulb goes out. I speak in torch and moonlight with the bowed shoulders of the hills as a back-drop.

Finish the evening as we always do with *Our* Pastor. Middle of nowhere. Middle of night. Car that won't start and the ten passengers pushing it. Home by 4:30. I think my body is broke too.

## 14<sup>th</sup> February 2001

Carlos asks us what *Brothel* is and Jeremy tells him that it is a place where prostitutes work. Carlos is shocked and says that the evangelist Smith Wigglesworth lived there. Turns out he means *Bradford*.

We book Carlos and Flor a room in a hotel for Valentine's Day. Fill it with flowers etc. Jeremy makes a smell in their sparkling clean bathroom just before they enter. Something beautiful about the expression on Jeremy's face at such moments of awkwardness.

Evening church service goes on for over three hours and people are falling over and twitching in the Holy Spirit right left and centre. Krysten is trying not to be scared. I have never once fallen over in the Spirit. I am secretly jealous of those who can. But when someone prays with a hand on my forehead and uses that hand to push me, I can't help but put one foot behind the other and push back. It's something in my nature I suppose. Though I am REALLY good at catching people.

## 17th February 2001

Church Camp since yesterday. A hundred people kneeling in prayer under the stars and this beautiful little black and white kitten appears under my poncho and stays there for the evening. Reading in a C.S. Lewis book about how we can reduce a moment of spiritual enlightenment to the bare physical facts. Namely looking at the stars with a cat in my poncho. If you analyse a moment of transcendence too much it disappears completely. Pop! And it is gone.

Round the fire tonight I tell a large group of fourteen-year-olds that I have the only toilet in Manchester and that the queues go around the block. I like to think that they will retain this information for years – then bring up the topic with the next British person they encounter. Long-sighted jokes are one of my favourite sorts.

Cannot shut the tent properly so the kitten gets in and keeps us awake all night by walking happily on our faces.

## 18th February 2001

Over-sweet coffee for breakfast, washed down by quiet time with God on the side of a hill. I have come a long way to get closer to God. Crossed an ocean. Followed a lot of instructions. Climbed a small hill. What is the difference between this hill and all the others I could have climbed?

## 20th February 2001

I am sitting alone on a pebbled beach enjoying some *espacio físi-co*. Watching the movement of people and waves. The sea draws me out of myself into something bigger. I could mention that someone just broke into the church and stole $1000 pesos (our return fare to Buenos Aires) but I have forgotten about that now – the sea is more interesting.

Try to get back into the church to sleep and hear strange noises coming from upstairs. Wonder if the robbers have come back – but then think that it is probably just the wind and the pigeons and Satan deliberately trying to scare us.

## 21st February 2001

Pray that our money will be found. Hear that the kids who took it have gone into the Surf Shop (run by someone from the church) and pay with $100 bills.

During evangelism I pray that God will lead me to the right people. I approach some kids just before Flor reaches them: rendered useless again because my Spanish still limits me. Talk to a woman who listens whilst looking elsewhere. And to another woman who has already accepted Jesus. Then to four little boys who are more interested in asking questions about Jeremy's fashion choices. Several teenagers on bikes appear from nowhere. Speak with as much passion as I can muster and wave my arms around a lot. Don't preach a sugar-coated gospel. Talk of the challenging lifestyle of love that Jesus calls us to. Sebastian accepts my message, can see by his eyes that he means it. Must have meant something for him to open up like that in front of his mates. Krysten sees my arm waving and calls me a dork. Beautiful thing to have someone from California call you a dork. Such an exotic word to us Brits. Still frustrated. Wish there were more practical things we could do to fill this city with love and give our words more substance.

## 22nd February 2001

Salmon at *a brother's* house for lunch and about five other types of meat including black pudding which I digest politely. I also digest it politely on behalf of other members of the team who are trying to find less immersive ways of being polite.

Just realised that my CDs were stolen as well as the money and Sarah's portable CD player. She had been so angry when it was taken and had said, "I hope yours gets stolen, so you know what it feels like." Well now I know. With everything that is taken from me I feel freer. Lighter. Less tied down. The less I have, the less I need. God, that sounds smug – I hate myself.

During intercession, we *claim* ten airplane tickets. We travelled here on bus, but we believe that God will redeem the missing money situation and that we will return in style. The pastor's son dreams that the church collects a big enough offering to fly him back to Buenos Aires too. He has a problem with his feet, and he needs to travel to the city to see a specialist. How do you know if a dream is from God or if it is wishful thinking? If I were God – I would fly him to Buenos Aires in style and make us walk.

## 24th February 2001

Sometimes I hate being a girl because I do not feel safe. During evangelism I got mobbed by a load of young boys, my watch gets smashed and they take one of my rings. When I eventually get back into the house in one piece, I burst into tears all over Mommy Flor, who still has not backed out of her decision to adopt me.

## 25th February 2001

$500 from the church collection and three watches. Mine stopped working completely so I get one of them, it belonged to Richard who is living in the church with us because his family does not have a house. I wonder if it is the only watch he has.

## 26th February 2001

A plane is the only way we could get back to Buenos Aires in time for graduation. Carlos has the idea of a Cargo Plane. Then Richard knocks on the door and comes in. Fran asks if he knows anyone in the army. The answer is yes. Fran, Richard and Carlos, have gone off in his car to the army base. We stay and pray. Sarah has a vision of a cream telephone with *extension 262* written on it. We check with the army, but they have no such number.

## 27th February 2001

Cargo Plane idea falls through. Shame. Having the Army fly three English people (so close to the Remembrance Day for the Falkland's War) and four illegal Latinos could have been fun.

More money collected. Carlos phones the airport. It is after hours so there is no answer. The recorded message asks him to enter the extension number if he has one. He enters 262. It works. We have tickets.

## 28th February 2001

On the plane about to take off. We don't think *Our* Pastor will make it to say goodbye, but he turns up in his usual way – with a slow engine rattle and seconds to spare.

Clouds are small and white, like speech bubbles with no words in them. Comodoro Rivadavia fades into the distance. A small brown land filled with colourful people, standing straight-backed to face the strong wind that sweeps their dusty city. The last scene I remember is of three churches standing together to wave us off. The tears they cry make me feel almost famous.

## 6th March 2001

Been back on the YWAM base in Buenos Aires for a few days now. Wonderful to say hello to the people I missed so much and sad to see so many of them returning to their home countries. I cry when Anna leaves. Maybe I will go and live with her in Jerusalem.

Been told that I will likely spend the next five months in the YWAM base run by Jorge Rios in Pringles.

## 12th March 2001

Brief holiday in Iguazu with Isabel. Giant iconic waterfalls drown out the voices of hundreds of admiring tourists, as if they do not care for compliments. Walk into the jungle in the evening. Giant blue morphos butterflies, toucans, and oversized termites. Sound of a twig snapping a few metres away. Freeze and slowly reach for each other's hands. Shared thoughts of big cats. Slowly become aware of a large family of *coatis*, who have shot up into trees at the first sight of us. Look at them and they look at us. Remain still until they decide that we are not real and slide slowly down the trees to carry on with their day, black and white tails swinging high behind them. Jog back, dodging giant webs and listening to howler monkeys. Isabel makes excellent monkey noises – she is good at things like that – but I am not sure that it is helpful. Two mile walk out of the forest, and three miles to town. Fully dark by now. Sound of bull frogs. Fire-flies like fallen stars in the grass. I connect their dots until the universe makes more sense and my heart is stitched back together by so many connecting lines.

## 18th March 2001

Back at the base. Go into Buenos Aires with Laura to watch tango dancing in *La Boca* (against the insanely colourful background of houses painted with paint left over from fishing boats). Attend a church service at *King of Kings* out of sheer curiosity. This mega-church was one of the hot spots in Argentina's spiritual revival and is a must see for any keen spiritual tourist. Pastored by Claudio Friezon, who started a congregation in a rough area of Belgrano after receiving a vision from The Lord. Meeting is a little manic. People enthusiastically attempting to receive anything God has on offer. Sermon is about determination to see God's face. Go forward for prayer, but cannot achieve the state of spiritual bliss that the rest of the congregation seem to be in. Distracted by the efficiency of the place: get prayed for, get pushed (sometimes very hard), fall over (in the power of the Holy Spirit), lie prostate on the floor twitching and speaking in tongues, get dragged to one side to make room for the next congregation who have been waiting noisily for the second service to start.

## 22nd March 2001

Reading *The Great Divorce* by C.S. Lewis. Love that his name is Clive Staples. Like what he says about art. That artists paint to share their glimpses of Heaven with others. But that when the real thing is before you, it has to be loved more than the weak copies you can make of it. I will remember this if I become an artist.

## 27th March 2001

Three-hour work duty with Anita from Brazil. She is small and black and round like a ball of Latino joy. Think she is teaching me Spanish, but it is Portuguese. Teach her to say, "Hello, I am Anita, your huggable friend. Squeeze my ear to receive your hug." She learns it well, apart from the fact that she pronounces *ear* as *rear* – which is unfortunate. Humour keeps me sane here. Leaving for four months in the Pringles YWAM base tomorrow. Run by Jorge, who used to be a member of *The Shining Path*. I am really not sure what to expect. In my bunk listening to music and the rain. Feeling the ebb of people coming and going, moving on, leaving behind, of autumn and of spring. Tightrope of the present stretched so thin between the weight of the past and future – it could snap at any moment. Falling asleep with the rainfall like a hundred eerie macumba drummers on the hollow objects outside.

I have never seen any of these drummers, but I often hear them at night. We are told that it is Brazilian witchcraft. Bad things do not seem to ever be Argentinian. If I ask too many questions, I am told that I am "very English," in a degrading tone. Am I being asked to preach The Kingdom of God or The Kingdom of Argentina? I don't know anymore. I left the United Kingdom because I wanted to be stateless – because I wanted to open my heart to the world – not because I wanted to form a new allegiance. I like being British – but they comment so often that I am starting to believe that my heritage is something shameful. I still believe that The Kingdom of God is hidden somewhere underneath all of this. There are so many frontiers to pick apart. Maybe I just need to leave Buenos Aires. Maybe the next town has something new to teach me.

CHAPTER 5

# Coronel Pringles

Jorge was born in the Amazonian city of Iquitos, the largest city in the world which is unreachable by road. He was given his first pair of shoes at thirteen. Two years later he joined the Peruvian army. After twenty-one jumps and three years as a paratrooper he left the army and started taking drugs. He opened his own lab and stayed in the drug business until he was twenty-five. This was when he had the first of his two conversion experiences and became a Marxist Communist and fighting member of *Sendero Luminoso* (The Shining Path) in the Peruvian Jungle. He was soon in command of hundreds.

In the dangerous Red Zone of this jungle lived the blind-accordion-playing-Pastor who led Jorge to God. The Pastor had lived here with his family for twelve years and Jorge was his only convert. Feeling like a new man, Jorge returned home for the first time in eight years to find that his sister, who should have been twenty-three, had just died of cancer. She was a Christian who had prayed for him ceaselessly.

One evening, whilst sitting with Jorge at his kitchen table in the Argentinean town of Coronel Pringles (named after an Argentine Colonel), he rolls up his sleeve to show us the hollow of a piranha bite. I press him for more stories, and he tells us of how he once wrestled a tiger – and won. He speaks conspiratorially of the giant pythons that are rumoured to live underground in the Rainforest – so big that they cause earthquakes when they move. Smiling awkwardly, he scratches at the little tuft of black hair that remains stubbornly at the front of his head after the rest has retreated. He is holding some stories back; there is a lot that he is not proud of. When preaching to us about Christian commitment Jorge once refers to the time when he ordered five suicide bombers to blow up an army command post – the youngest was a girl of thirteen.

Then – with eyes that have softened rather than hardened under the weight of pain – he pulls out a photo of his daughter Laura and a news clipping of the coach accident in which she died as a baby. His Argentinean wife, Isabel, was badly injured, but has recovered. This happened several years before my arrival on their little missionary base. Though in reality it is little more than their small home, surrounded ambitiously by a few piles of bricks that we are told will become more buildings. I am sure they will; Jorge is a man who does not back down easily. I am uncertain if the fact that he keeps reminding us not to fear him does much to ease my comfort.

We are interrupted by Juliana from Brazil, stomping through the kitchen on her way to our bedroom. She is back from the library. I find her sitting sullenly on her top bunk under the banner of letters that she has spent hours colouring lovingly in. J.E.S.U.S. Last night Juli dreamed that God was sending her to Bhutan. She did not know where Bhutan was and went to look it up in a book. It was a surprise.

"Bhutan only has three aeroplanes," she tells me. "You're not allowed in if you're a Christian. It's going to be very difficult."

"Shall we go buy some cheese and talk about it?" Cheese has always been her crutch in times of crisis.

The streets of Pringles are bright and crisp in the winter light. I am proud of myself for keeping up with her rapid Spanish as she animatedly tells about how she has just led Norberto to the Lord. He is a well-known local character who lives in the graveyard. I tread carefully over the uneven cobbled stones as we walk, remembering with pain a home visit I had made with Jorge a week previously. I politely drank more *mate* than my bladder could hold and the bicycle ride home over the cobbles was agony. We buy our cheese from a jumbled little kiosk.

"I'll have a spot in the morning if I eat all this," she sighs.

We save the cheese for later and stay to have coffee in *Café Lucas* before returning to do our YWAM work duties. Juliana fascinates me. Today she is clown-like in her red dungarees and yellow trainers. When she wants, she can dress like a film star. Now, the only thing making her shine are the eyes that watch me like planets rising over the rim of her cup.

"I don't know how I'll cope on the base with only Isabel." Her eyes, as round and black as the surface of her coffee, are rippling with tears. I will leave in two weeks and her greatest fear is that of being alone. When first arriving to serve the Lord in Argentina Juliana had preached about how God is the Potter and we are the clay. Since then she claims that her life has been a parade of family deaths and personal tragedies. Marriage to an Englishman had been on the horizon, when the relationship had broken down and she had escaped to recover in Pringles. Gripping the cup in her hands she tells me how God uses suffering to mould us into something beautiful.

"You know, when he presses his fingers inside and pushes the clay out. It hurts. But it gives you shape. You are already dizzy from spinning on the wheel and think he must be nearly finished, when he spots a crack, squashes you back to nothing and begins again. This is the brokenness of the spirit that he uses to build us up. Then we are complete. But he needs to put us in the oven to make us strong. That hurts more than anything." She is crying now, her eyes searching mine as if she is looking for a way to pour some of herself into them. "So, we are out of the oven. Finished? No! We have no colour. We need to be glazed." Her long fingers smooth over the coffee cup. "Back in the oven. The temperature's so high it's likely we will crack. But we don't. He is a good Potter. Finished? No! Another layer of glaze and back in the oven. We have given up by now, for sure. Then, gradually our eyes adjust the light as the oven door opens. Though, to be honest Emily, I don't know if it will ever end."

I am crying too by now. From the sheer exhaustion of it all. From the pain of having had virtually no control over my own life for the past ten months. From the constant emotional amputation caused by growing so close to so many people that they became like my own flesh, only to have them leave after a few months, and possibly forever. It is not a moment to rush past, but slowly, as we look at each other's faces - we start to laugh. A mad laughter that makes a few customers turn and stare. Laughter and tears together. Sun and rain. I look around for a rainbow.

# Liberating Demonised Cats

Walking back, we pass an old gaucho leaning an arm on the side of his horse drawn cart. A tiny black and tan pup stands with trembling legs near his feet. He nods to us,

"Buenos dias."

"I prefer dogs to cats," says Juliana with a wink after we have passed.

"I've gone off them too. I'm going to miss you Juli, when I'm in England and I see a demonised cat and there's no one to save me."

She rears up, waving her arms in impersonation of the cat we refer to. We had been sent to pray outside the house of an ex-witch – a woman called Adriana who swore that a coven sent an evil white cat to spy on her.

No one was home when we arrived, so – we waited. Then waited some more. We had walked a very long way to get there. Eventually we gave in and decided to leave – but prayed quickly before doing so. Almost as soon as we opened our mouths, we spotted a beautiful white feline leaping through the long grass in the distance. It was headed straight towards us. We did our best to ignore its direct gaze and prayed a blessing on the house. As we prayed blessings over the doors and windows, the cat followed and rubbed its scent against the same spots – as if to reclaim the house for Satan. We rebuked it in the name of Jesus, and it reared up on its hind legs – never ceasing to look us in the eyes. White, elegant, and distinctly evil. Juli and I faced it holding hands – perhaps the only sensible thing to do in such a situation. Maybe the only way for any of us to face anything scary is to hold hands and shout verses from the Bible.

There are many more diary entries covering my time in Argentina, reading them has exhausted me, and I would not like to exhaust you further by continuing to expose you to such content. Pages are crammed with Bible verses and a stream-of-consciousness-like-critique-of-spiritual-performance. Wish I could reach inside the pages to tell myself to breathe a few times. Wish I could tell myself that I was a teenager. That teenagers are allowed to cut themselves some slack.

Anything after my time in Pringles would be a hard adjustment. I had been working for a converted terrorist who had redirected all of his radical views towards the Christian cause. I had been visiting and preaching in local churches in a rural community where it was normal to keep an armadillo in a barrel and a cow's head on a hook in the kitchen.

I return to the UK for a year where I study art and preach in local churches. Then, when the pain of normality becomes more than I can bear, I return to Argentina for a further three years where I work in YWAM discipleship schools and in an arts group in a giant warehouse in the centre of Buenos Aires.

The real occurrences in my life during this time do not happen during the big events, but in the small gaps between them. The church meetings and big Christian rallies are not the places where I have life changing experiences. Instead, it is on my days off and during my holidays – when I am far from organisations and institutions – that I feel free enough to be sure that the experiences I have are unfabricated. These are the stories that I am going to tell you now.

CHAPTER 6

# Hitchhiking with Drug Dealers in Uruguay

I am living with dozens of zealous young people in a missionary community in Buenos Aires. My mother still calls from England to check I am reading my Bible and going to church on Sundays. Quiet time with God is a scheduled part of my morning routine. The pressure I am putting on myself to perform spiritually makes me feel like I am part of the Christian Olympics.

I leave it all behind for an impromptu trip to Uruguay. Leave my credit card and grab a handful of cash. Take nothing but a small tent, a box of jewellery making equipment, and two friends. The heat, and the weight of my bag makes the place between my shoulder blades itch. Buds of wings wanting to open and quiver in the sunlight. An innate call towards flight battling the pull of the ground.

A bus takes us to the ferry port, dusty sprawl of Buenos Aires swirling past. My cheek presses to the glass trying to absorb the city's memory of wide-open plains sighing in surrender as the Spaniards ride in to tame them. We pool our resources at the ticket counter – realising that we do not have enough money for our return ferry tickets. The pause lasts two seconds, folded wings twitching under our back-backs – we exhale – and push the money across the counter.

The depth of our commitment does not sink in until we are in the middle of the Rio de la Plata Estuary and the only country visible is Uruguay. The world's widest river. Somewhere beneath us rests the wreck of the Admiral Graf Spee – a German ship sunk on the site of World War Two's first naval battle. I imagine its reincarnated form, kingdom of the rare La Plata dolphin and the leatherback sea turtle. Possessions have fallen away like ballast since leaving England, now down to one small bag, I am buoyant enough to float. This location feels like privilege. I am undercover. Trying on an alternative heritage for size. Standing there on the deck, sandwiched between my Brazilian friend Kika and Yanina from Argentina. I have invaded the continent like that war ship, been engulfed into it. Swallowed up. Accepted enough for a turtle to swim by without raising an eyebrow.

Colonia de Sacramento has buildings dating back to 1680, the year the Port is founded by the Portuguese. Cobbled lanes are lined with half-hidden shops selling homemade ice cream and handcrafted souvenirs. We do not care about these things – Yanina's thermos flask is empty and we need hot water to make *mate*. No Argentinian can last more than a few hours without a drink from the communal-herb-filled-gourd. Eventually, we find a service station on the edge of town with a machine dispensing free hot water. Like the indigenous people who survive a famine because of the nourishing properties of their national drink – we are saved. We sit on an upturned boat abandoned by the roadside and take turns filtering the warm smoky liquid through its metal straw.

"Should we find a campsite?" my mind is already rolling out its sleeping bag.

"Too expensive" says Kika, "tourist prices."

I think of the boat we are sitting on, but I am not sure about waking up on a traffic island. Then I imagine us sleeping in a shop doorway and getting moved by a policeman who is trying to keep things nice for tourists. Kika tucks back that one little rebellious dreadlock, and points to the sign in front of us: *Highway 1 East to Montevideo.*

"We'll hitch."

After refilling the thermos, we stroll through the parched grass at the roadside. Thumbs out. No cars are stopping. We sing, we dance, we smile. We walk in a way that makes us look approachable but not vulnerable. They are still not stopping. *Maybe people don't do this in Uruguay?* The sun is slipping down like our spirits through light-fingered clouds, the dirt orange in its tail lights. We have walked a mile or more. Yanina kneels in the dust to pray, shaking her fist at the heavens in angry laughter. A blue van passes us and stops. *Does he think that the fist shaking is aimed at him?* We freeze, not knowing which way to run. He opens his door and beckons us with a grin.

Roberto lectures us for the first few miles – "girls travelling alone should be more careful, anyone could have picked you up." Uruguay pours past the window, flat fields and ranches on replay – until we make an unexpected turn and bump up to wait outside a house, dogs barking. Our driver talks in low tones to a man outside. Money slips from one hand to another. *Drugs?* Glancing at each other we make a silent pact not to mention this to our leaders back in Buenos Aires. What could we do about it? Still eighty miles from Montevideo. We have to trust the God that we read about in books.

Dusk is now red on our tail as we near the capital. Roberto says we can spend the night in his family home. I shake my head – I have heard the stories. Though I know in the part of me that is not my brain that he is a good man. I sense Kika and Yanina think that his idea is better than the alternative. I see the worry in his unshaven face as he leaves us at the gaping mouth of the bus station and realise instantly that I have made a mistake. Roberto returns an hour later to buy us steaming hot doughnuts from one of the station's vendors. He does not repeat his offer, and we do not think to ask him to.

Our corner of the Tres Cruses bus station smells of tired travellers and sizzling chori-pan. I take a bag of cashews from my rucksack. My Mother has posted them from England, even though I tell her that we have nuts in South America. I cram a handful in my mouth.

"The leaders will go crazy if they find out we hitched. I promised them we wouldn't." Kika's Brazilian accent adds a dramatic musical strain to the words.

I burst into tears. My face is the Iguazu waterfalls, the rivers of three countries joining in frothy turmoil. It is not because all this scares me – quite the opposite – *How can this be wrong?* How can it be unwise to place your life squarely into the hands of God? To feel inside yourself that you are flying – your soul returning home like a caged parrot to the jungle. My world sways as I balance the question in my mind. Tears subside eventually and I am left as brittle as dried salt: the salty cashews in my mouth, the salt-carved paths on a dirty face and the smell of the sea in my hair.

I have spent decades trying to prop up my faith with second-hand certainty. Now I am trying to kick away that certainty in order to give my faith space to breathe. This salty moment at the bus terminal is when I start to cross over the parted sea between the lands of faith and doubt – inviting the water to seal the gap behind me. I do not understand all of this yet, but the beautiful pain of the moment lies heavy on me, a giant palm of pressure, ready to both protect and push me into the great unknowing.

Rain washes down the outside of the large glass windows and cold air flushes through the terminal every time the sliding doors open. Yanina looks down at her exposed toes in the flip-flops that had been plenty warm enough in Argentina.

"My feet are freezing."

Our last five pesos are spent on socks for her to wear with them. We are not as well prepared as the now thinning stream of tourists who file resolutely past.

"Look at him" says Kika, pointing at a man burdened under the weight of his camera equipment. "Looks like he's in a hurry to get to his next location. Bet he's got a book called Ten Great Photos You Must Take in South America or something. You know that phrase, the journey is the destination? I wonder if he heard it."

She pulls out a camera and we laugh, giddy with exhaustion, as she takes a photo of Yanina's feet. Settling in an out-of-the-way spot, we lie down in our sleeping bags. The second we are comfortable a security guard curtly informs us that we cannot sleep in the terminal. He points us to a row of smooth ugly yellow chairs with raised arms and low backs. By the morning we have managed only a few moments of sleep; heads resting on each other's shoulders and in a variety of other impossible positions.

Our new day has a new goal – sleep. We walk. I follow Kika, an overgrown duckling twice her size. Sometimes I watch myself from an outside perspective – like I am a character in a book or an actor in a movie. I enjoy doing this. At least something interesting is happening. At least I am not sitting in my parent's house staring at the ceiling. The self-imposed glass frontage of a church blinks at us from the middle of a block of grey buildings. It is Monday and the doors are shut, but a shadow moves inside; a woman is vacuuming. We ring the bell. Twice. Three times. She opens the door slowly, distrustfully.

"Si?"

We explain that we are holidaying missionaries caught in a spot of bother. Her thick hands smooth her apron.

"Well... the soup kitchen, that's open today I guess."

It is forty blocks away and the rain is still pouring. We wash up at a crumbling colonial building half hidden by a tree that splits the pavement as it grows. We go in and make a deal – we will help cook for the hungry in exchange for food and a bed for the night. They are understaffed and glad of the help. Vegetables boil in dented silver cauldrons. The sort of meal you can add water to if more people arrive – and they do: old men, drunks, children, families. Some with faces as grey as their clothes, others talking gaily as if in a queue for the movies. It is 2001 and Uruguay – despite being one of the richest countries in Latin America – has succumbed to the tremors spreading from Argentina's economic earthquake. I don't want to think too hard about what this means for them. I sit at the top of the stairs and re-centre myself by stroking a tiny black and white kitten that is being trained up to catch mice. He purrs, oblivious to the world's problems, and squints his cloudless blue eyes.

That night – on rattling fold-out beds – is one of glorious horizontal bliss. We wake ready to hit the road. After refusing a lift from a battered car jammed full of hormone-fuelled adolescents (who say we can sit on their knees), we find a ride with a doctor in a shiny blue Peugeot. We drive along the coast feeling rich and privileged. Thirty miles later we thank him for his lecture on the dangers of hitchhiking, and he leaves us on the beach of a coastal town called Atlantida (Spanish for Atlantis). We are on the edge of the pueblo, the area where the real people live – not where tourists go. We like it here. It is the thirty-first of December, this is where we will celebrate New Year. Walking down the beach we comb the white sand with our toes, looking for shells. I fill my pockets with pieces of coloured glass rounded into pebbles by the sea. I called them jewels as child, marvelling at the way the rough sea made them smooth.

A few blocks from the beach is a supermarket called *La Inglesa* (The English Girl). We sit outside it all day in the sun making jewellery from our beach combings. Kika sings a song that roughly translates into English as *shake off your bitterness and buy an ankle bracelet*. The song is not great – but her voice is. I don't know how, but we make enough money not only to buy cheap cider and a modest feast to welcome in the New Year, but also to return to Colonia by coach. We even have enough for the ferry.

Evening approaches and we assemble our flimsy tent, hiding it as well as we can under the cover of trees at the top of the beach. After toasting in the year with a shared bottle, I walk into the sea to watch the fireworks rain over Montevideo. The water is alive with borrowed colour that dances under the waves. Flares from a submerged city forgotten by everyone but me. The explosions subside enough for the stars to show their features. I stand with a naked soul and stare the universe in its unfamiliar face. Shifting my gaze, I look deep into my watery reflection and consider the woman who longs to be lifted dripping from the sea. A woman half-drowned by the weight of false certainty, waiting to be reborn through salty baptism. Her mind smooth and clean, broken edges worn down by the experience of having an open heart, on an open road.

Arriving back in Colonia the next day we realise we have miscalculated the conversion rate of Uruguayan to Argentinean pesos – we are twenty short for the Ferry. In the port, I approach a couple of middle-class Scottish tourists with a bracelet made from worn sea glass, explaining our predicament. Their hard look reminds me that I have crossed over. A young English woman with skin now as dark as any Latino. I am one of those strange others – the sort of person that civilised people don't talk to.

We have two hours to make twenty pesos. *How could we have made such a simple mistake?* How have we managed to survive on only faith and *mate* for the past three days only to fall at the last hurdle? We slump dejected on a bench at the top of the beach.

"Just one last miracle please God." I overhear Yanina mutter.

"Wait!" I say, "isn't that–"

"–Franchesca" says Kika

Gazing out to sea at the water's edge is the leader of my Outreach to Comodoro Rivadavia – here to renew her three-month tourist visa. We hug her in relief and (without expanding our story in too much detail) ask to borrow money.

CHAPTER 7

# Hitchhiking with Drunken Nuns

We live in a whirlpool of Christian charisma – the arm waving and hand clapping make me dizzy. From my reserved British perspective there is an excessive amount of noise. To counteract this, I start attending an English-speaking church that my American friend Quel has found in the leafy upper-class district of Acassuso. It is perfect. The liturgy is short and sweet, the congregation are polite, and mostly American. They serve regular pot-luck lunches that taste of a home I miss but have never been to.

It is on one of these occasions that we meet Marie, an old woman of English heritage, whose father had settled in Argentina about a hundred years ago. We mention that we want to escape Buenos Aires over Christmas and are looking for a place in Patagonia where we can pitch our tent. That is easy, she says, she owns land near Junín de Los Andes.

Quel, Jeremy and I travel on a coach that does not stop when it hits a dog – and later decides to stop and wait in the middle of the road for twelve hours for no apparent reason. The air conditioning is absent during the scorching heat of the day and appears at full strength in the evening – making sleep impossible. We are promised food and a movie – and are given neither. We make another long stop where the driver shouts so much at the steward that he leaves crying. The driver is replaced, and the new steward is emotionally stable enough to provide us with food and water.

After a night in San Martín de Los Andes we take a bus to Junín. It is more of a van than a bus, driven by a jovial character with unbelievably long arm hair. When the other passengers have been dropped off, he asks if we would like to visit a friend of his on the way.

Kay and her daughter Grace live in a Tiny House. I don't mean that it is small – I mean that it is about the size of a large garden shed. Kay is from Massachusetts and has been stranded in this remote town since the dissolution of her marriage to an Argentinian eleven years previously. They appreciate the visit from a fellow American – especially when Quel pulls a packet of cranberries out of her backpack. It is Christmas Day tomorrow, and Grace has never tried them. Meeting them is providential. We have been unable to make telephone contact with Marie, and Kay gives us a number of a mutual friend.

We call her when we reach the town and are told that Marie is recovering from a heart attack in Buenos Aires and will not make it to Junín for Christmas. We call her at her daughter's home to wish her a speedy recovery. She insists that we still camp at La Estancia de los Helechos – saying that the only way to find it is to look for a taxi driver called Miguel in the town square. There are tens of taxi drivers stationed around a sizeable square. We go ahead foolishly and ask the nearest one if he knows of a Miguel. He says that he himself is that Miguel, and that he knows exactly where to take us.

He drives us west towards the Andes. The eternally snow-capped volcano Lanín hugs the horizon like He owns it. We head up a track along the shore of lake Huechulafquen, Miguel talks as he drives. He points out a small village named after Marie's father, and then at a mountain named after her grandfather. She has under-stated the amount of land she owns. Eventually we stop in a place that is so far from all other places, that it really is not a place at all. It is more of an anywhere, on the edge of a nowhere – a few miles beyond one of the forgotten toes splayed out by the Great Mountain Range that separates us from Chile. Miguel helps us unload our bags and drives away in a haze of red earth like a genie returning to a bottle. There is no civilization within sight. The only life we can see is a large bull – who is closer to our camping spot than we appreciate.

It is Christmas 2003, and we are starting to realise that we are not well prepared for it. Jeremy has forgotten his tent poles. The only provisions we have with us are dried beans, eggs, some pork and a bottle of Pina Colada. We improvise. Shoelaces tie the tent to trees, scraps of pork are cooked on sticks over an open fire, and beans are boiled for hours and hours until they are soft enough to eat – I have had more disappointing Christmases. I keep the Pina Colada cool by floating it in the lake, and my sleeping bag warm with one of the hot stones from the fire. We take it in turns to read Wuthering Heights out loud, falling asleep to whispers of *Cathy*, as trees reach to brush their long fingers together over our heads.

We wake early on Boxing Day and improvise a breakfast of eggs cooked in a cake pan. We then set out to find the Mapuche-Indian community rumoured to be located somewhere in the direction of the volcano. We walk until we have blisters on every toe of both feet. We walk until the volcano should be the only thing filling our vision – but He is shrouded in cloud and invisible to us. He is watching though; we can sense it. The same thing happens with the Indigenous population. We see no one but are aware of our conspicuous presence in the landscape. Only evidence we find of the Mapuche Settlement is a little boy trying to sell us flies and a small wooden cafe with fish hanging to dry on the porch. We do not recognise its owner as Mapuche at first – a beautiful elderly woman with skin creased and folded like the hills.

We start to head back, walking under the dark canopy of trees. The wind and the rain are both forces to be reckoned with in the high altitude cold of early summer in the Andes. Little streams trickle past us through moss covered rocks. We walk until we see where Huechulafquen splits into two smaller lakes: Paimun and Epulafquen. The presence of Lanín looms sleepily behind us from beneath his blanket of cloud. We think about the young princess who is hidden somewhere in his belly after being dropped there by a condor to appease Him when He erupted because of the hunting on His slopes. Locals have learnt that the Lanín National Park is an area where nature is to be respected. He is not the sort of volcano you would want to offend. The cloud over Him has grown darker, but ahead of us we see a gap in the weather and the giant smile of a rainbow reaching down to kiss the surface of the lake. Our spirits are lifted. Coloured light skips down the mountainsides and dances over the water. Then – as if part of some great orchestrated finale – an old Gaucho rides by in full traditional dress. He winks at us – the land tells him secrets that he is not allowed to share.

The next day, after a lunch of beans in spicy ketchup and a few unexpected bits of sand, we pack up camp and head back towards civilisation. Our blistered feet raw under the weight of our bags. We walk a long way before realising that civilisation is in the other direction. We realise something else – we do not want to do any more walking. We decide to hitch – a futile idea really, seeing as we have not seen a car all day. Quel prays, "God, we'd like a car to stop for us soon. And just to be clear God. I mean soon as we understand it, not as you understand it. I know that our concepts of time are slightly different." And – almost as she finishes praying – one does.

We continue our journey south of Junín by coach and arrive back in the picturesque town of San Martín de Los Andes. From here we take a further coach, following the shore of the glacial Lake Lácar until we cross the border into Chile. From there we take a ferry up the mountain-enclosed lake Pirihueico. Disembarking, we immediately fall in love with the small town of Puerto Fuy and set up home in a hostel.

Jeremy and Quel set off one morning to visit the Huilo Huilo waterfalls. I want to go too, but do not fancy another long walk. I am sitting by the lake's shore communing with the Andes, when I notice some kids playing with a bike that is far too big for them. South-American children are very easy to talk to – soon I am taken back to where their mother is working in the port's bakery. I ask her if she will let them rent me the bicycle. She does. Cycling is a lot quicker than walking, and soon I have joined my friends for a day spent by the magical waterfalls. On my return I am met by an excited huddle of children – animatedly discussing the logistics of starting a bicycle-based tourist business.

On our last day we are eating the only meal on the menu of the pueblo's only restaurant. I just love that their English translation for granary bread roll is "brown bread in uproar". I am wondering if it

would be improper to steal a menu, when my attention is drawn to
our fellow diners. A family of nuns are drinking beer and laughing
like school girls. Such a beautiful sisterhood. Makes me feel jealous
for a moment. Makes me want to ask if they have a spare habit so I
can join their table.

We realise during the meal that we have made a vital mistake.
We have not checked the bus timetable, and there isn't one today.
We need to leave right away to catch our coach from San Martín
to Buenos Aires. After approaching the problem from all the angles
that it has – and some that it does not – we decide that our only
option is to hitchhike again. There are six vehicles already board-
ing the last ferry; our destiny is in their hands. Most of the cars are
full of baggage and passengers, though Quel manages to get a lift
with a van full of kayaking tourists from New Mexico. There is one
truck left; its seats taken up by the nuns from the restaurant who are
returning from their holiday in an increasingly jovial mood. Doing
the charitable thing comes naturally to them – they let Jeremy and
I sit in the back with their luggage.

This location gives us a chance to observe, without them being
too aware of our presence. They operate like a family unit. The older women mother and chastise the youngest of the five, who seems
to be the one who has had the most to drink. My favourite moment
is going through customs with them at the border between Chile
and Argentina.

"Did you pack your bags yourselves? Is there anything in your
trunk that you want to declare?"

"Well there are two British people, but they got in of their own
accord."

It is not their status as nuns that prevent the women from getting searched – it is the expression on their faces. *We don't care what country you think you represent; we are sent by a higher authority.* They switch between their private and public personas quickly. No hint of frivolity is present, and all tipsiness corked until we are back in the car.

We are dropped off outside their orphanage in San Martín de los Andes. When we kiss them goodbye, I feel like curtseying. I enjoyed travelling with the nuns far more than I would have enjoyed traveling by bus. I decide to accept this dynamic – life's missed busses will no longer be perceived as road blocks to some allegedly perfect plan. A missed bus will become a new opportunity. When I screw up and am forced to find an alternative solution, the Great Mystery of Life will cups its hands together to pool its resources. Mistakes will be bridges into mystery. Wrong turns will be roads to unexpected destiny. Failure will lead me to admit the degree to which I need other people, and the degree to which I enjoy their company.

So many strange things happened during my ensuing years in South America that they have all blurred into one - I remember a mentally ill student coming into the kitchen whilst I was cooking and demanding that I give him a knife to kill a snake. I remember Quel spending several hours cleaning the white marks off a bush in the garden as a punishment for her rebellious attitude. I remember leading a team in Southern Chile and praying for food seconds before The Salvation Army entered carrying bags of provisions. I remember a young American confusing the words peine and pene

– and asking a dorm full of blushing girls if they have seen his penis, when he meant hairbrush. I remember Jeremy confusing the words remera and ramera – and telling some respectable church ladies that he had been so cold at night that he had slept with a whore, when he meant T-shirt. I remember hitchhiking in a van proudly labelled Firemen which contained nothing but an empty bucket. I remember hearing people talk in strange voices as they were liberated from demons. I remember riding bare-backed with gauchos to round up cattle. I remember being in a building that was shot at as thieves stole one of our cars. I remember that those who left were spoken about in hushed tones. I remember an old Chilean lady feeding us on nothing but cake because she thought that was what Gringos ate. I remember enjoying a lovely meal and being told afterwards that we had eaten horse. I remember being asked to preach in large churches with two minutes notice. I remember diving off a bridge into a river in Bolivia and all my clothes exploding. I remember working like a sleep deprived maniac to turn an abandoned warehouse into a huge art exhibition. I remember an outreach with dozens of Argentineans which resulted in me spending several months of my life dressed as a man for a play about South America at the Edinburgh Fringe Festival.

It is during this time – when I have a moustache and am wearing oversized men's dress shoes – that I start a relationship with my soon-to-be Argentinian husband Diego. We had first met when a group of us went to juggle in a park in Buenos Aires. He made me laugh. That was all it took. I was so very tired of the seriousness of everything that all I wanted to do was to laugh – to throw my head back and forget where I was for a second. There were very few men in Argentina who were taller than me – my options were narrow, but Diego was funny and charismatic. He enjoyed the company of other people enough for the prospect of a relationship not to feel claustrophobic. I just wanted to have some fun.

YWAM Argentina has an interesting policy on relationships: To ensure maximum holiness, dating is changed into something called *special friendship* where no physical contact is allowed – Diego and I are reprimanded for walking too close together as our troop traverses Edinburgh on our way to perform. Special Friendship is a time when the couple are encouraged to pray and seek God regarding their union. If marriage is deemed to be God's will a second phase is entered. That phase is called *Noviazgo*, and it means that the couple are engaged to be married. After spending my whole life single and devoted to God, I really want to date – but I only get to do so for about five minutes.

Diego sells his guitar and presents me with a simple gold ring in a Buenos Aires café. I am confused not only by YWAM's courtship tradition, but also by Argentina's – they put the ring on the right hand and move it to the left when they are married. I am engaged before I am fully aware of what is happening. I look down at the ring on my right hand and wonder if an engagement on the other side of the world, and the other side of my body will make my whole marriage feel like an attempt to read a book from right to left. But new beginnings are in store, no matter what direction they come from.

CHAPTER 8

# The Walls Fall Down

I should not have been surprised by anything that was about to happen – you would think the dream I had before leaving missionary life in Argentina would have given me some clues.

*I am standing in the centre of an ancient courtyard enclosed by thick, corroded limestone walls, when I hear a distant roar approaching like a tidal wave of sound. The ground convulses. Dust billows around me like a living cocoon. The walls scream to the ground and become rubble.*

Without knowing about the dream, the following day two people present me with this Bible verse: *In a little while I will once more shake the heavens and the earth... The glory of this new temple will be greater than the glory of the former – Haggai 2:6-9.* Someone else has a vision of an earthquake. Several more people sense that change is in the air for me. I of course think that all of this is wonderful. My second-hand-certainty is going to be demolished to make way for a new super-faith highway. My Christianity will no longer be accommodation rented out from my spiritual superiors. Whatever is built in its place will be fully mine. I will reside there, happy in the knowledge that I have finally found a stable home.

I am wrong.

I write this poem about the remodelling that starts to take place in my heart on that day.

## Walls

*For two decades I sit in churches on sunny days*
*The world outside further away*
*Than the time-locked saints on the stained-glass windows.*
*The sun's light falls on me*
*Through their tinted halos*
*And I stretch out my toes*
*In the borrowed light of transcendence.*

*Until one day I dream*
*That I hear the earth roaring*
*And see the great stones of the temple falling*
*Down around me.*
*I am left exposed and cold,*
*Because the truths that have been my childhood friends*
*Have grown old and grey,*
*While I have stayed*
*Young.*

*And I stand in the same spot for years,*
*Staring in shellshock at the broken walls*
*Waiting for it to be rebuilt.*
*Because I was told that the glory of the first temple*
*Will be nothing compared to the glory of the new.*

*But they never came to understand glory in the way that I now do.*
*I stop regarding the rubble*
*And notice I can see the sky*
*Bending down to reach me*
*Like a hug from otherness in a gown of blue.*
*I stop looking down in frustration*
*At the empty page I have come to be*
*And see instead before me the unbearable beauty*
*Of a new-born blanket of snow.*
*Walls*
*Are the opposite of bridges*
*Walls*
*Are arguments you're determined to win*
*Walls*
*Are built to keep you safe*
*Walls*
*Are built to keep you in.*

I do not understand the full significance of the dream straight away. I do not understand that God will not knock down one structure only to build another. I do not understand that my religious ideologies are walls I am trapped by. I do not understand that so much ugly doctrine has been woven into a Jesus coloured rug under which everything has been swept. I do not understand that once you lift the rug you cannot un-see what you have seen. I do not understand that you cannot put the lid back on a building that no longer has walls. *Don't you know that you yourselves are God's temple and that God's Spirit dwells in your midst? – 1 Corinthians 3:6.*

Instead of embracing the beauty of the white page that I have become, I spend a few more years rolling in the painful rubble of my post-Christendom, putting one rock on top of another and watching them topple.

Most of the leaders are in different countries leading outreaches when Diego and I decide to leave. I am temporarily in charge of the massive warehouse in the centre of Buenos Aires and Diego is responsible for the building that runs communications and media schools a few blocks away. As soon as one of the leaders returns, we tell her of our plans. She is kind to us; says she is sad to see us go but that we have her support. A day later she approaches with a different tone of voice and bundles us into her car to drive us to the main YWAM base on the outskirts of the city. A room full of high-rank leaders are waiting like dragons in a small circle that curls around us. We have stepped out from under their spiritual cover and God will not be pleased. They graciously allow us to leave, but withhold their blessing. Without them close at hand they believe that it is highly likely that we will fall into sexual sin before marriage. They give us long pitying looks and glance knowingly at each other.

I don't let my emotions show. My foundation has crumbled. I am the child who did everything asked of me. For five years I gave all of my money, all of my time, all of my energy. I look up to these leaders as if they are family. I want a hug. I want to know that they love and support me whatever I chose to do. Leaving without their blessing confuses me on a deep level. What have I done wrong? I do not want to leave to live a life of sin. I want to do all of the right things. I want to do whatever is true. I want nothing other than to follow a path of love. What confuses me more than anything is that

I cannot sense any of that love coming from them, and I had sincerely thought that they were better than that.

*Have I just seen behind the curtain? Is this the spirit at the heart of it all? Is this the face that meets anyone who steps out of line? Was it never about love? Has it been about power all along? What if I had not been strong enough to stand up and leave that room? What would have happened then? What will happen to those who won't leave to follow their dreams? Will they become life-long slaves to the dreams of others?*

I buy a simple dress before leaving Argentina, and a Derbyshire farmer lets us use his barn as a stunning location for celebrations. I am married before I know it. I enjoy our beautiful British wedding day – my happiness an act of defiance against the cross-cultural tensions that threaten to destroy everything. My mother wringing her hands. Diego in a pair of rented shoes that are too big for him.

*How did I get here? Did I make these decisions? Is the Will of The Divine some great cosmic river washing me to the sea?*

Shortly afterwards, Diego and I follow *the voice of God* and move to the Youth With A Mission base in Amsterdam. We make a grand entrance – waiting for streamers and applause – and slowly become aware that they are not expecting us. The person we have communicated with has forgotten to tell anyone. It is a relaxed environment; sometimes we float around almost aimlessly. We are told to rest after our work is finished – in Argentina working in our free time is how we show our true commitment to God. Armando (the base director) makes us feel like family. He is a Jewish man from Venezuela with broad shoulders and an even broader smile. We are often invited into his Moroccan style living room for Shabbat festivities. A space embodied by the Dutch word for a cosy and relaxed social situation – *gezelligheid*.

*Is it the warmth of a family home that I have longed for all along? Is that what I am travelling the world to find? Am I pretending to save the world, when all I really want is for the world to save me?*

Diego and I are eventually given a small room in the YWAM building, an old Mariner's Hotel overlooking a beautiful harbour. Warm light flickers like candles on the water as I sit on our double loft bed, trying to make sense of the world through our tiny window.

*Does God really want us here? What were we trying to achieve?*

We are staff on the Discipleship Training School. It is fun to feel young and free in such a beautiful city. Once, we steal a rowing boat that has been left half-submerged and tour the city's canals, returning it in better condition when our consciences become unsettled. Living on the base is like being in university halls of residence. Practical jokes sometimes take precedent over spiritual development. A firm hand is needed to check things run to schedule. I am asked to ensure that people reach the classrooms on time. A Chinese student called Forest is often late, and to my dismay I find myself saying the words *run, Forest. Run!* to hasten him along. Time moves faster than Forest; the antics of the school recede to make way for The Outreach.

*What can I possibly have taught these students? When I*
*ask the universe to reveal its truth to me all I hear is the*
*quiet hum of the planets asking each other questions.*

The team that we lead is a social experiment that makes the twelve disciples look like trained professionals. There is Nölani: a Canadian artist with green hair, Kala: a Croatian with a lot of very strange and very strong opinions, Silas: a quiet Brazilian musician, Gul and Kaleem: two beautiful turbaned and bearded pastors from Pakistan, John and Jacqueline and their three teenage children: a loving Australian family, Nathan: a cheeky New Zealander, Stefan: the son of a South African Pastor, and last but not least – Abayomrunkoje: an unbalanced Nigerian prince who is supposed to be co-leading the team with us.

*Why has so much money had been donated by local*
*churches to pay for this trip? What sort of a message of*
*hope could fly in for two months and then leave?*

I can smell the exact ingredients of the spicy food that Abayomrunkoje smuggles onto the plane from several rows away. It is the first hint that I am pregnant. We had looked into the big brown eyes of a beautiful Mexican baby called Ian on the base in Amsterdam and decided we wanted one too.

*Is making Christian babies more effective than evangelism?*
*If I was God would I want more Christians?*

My first mistake is to assume that morning sickness is limited to the morning. Something that can be briefly acknowledged on waking, before fading enough for breakfast to be enjoyed with relish. I am wrong. I have not done my research. Google had been invented eight years previously, but I have not yet learnt how to use it properly. I know none of the things that people should know before deciding to have babies.

We arrive safely in Caracas, but our bags do not. A minor issue compared to the other things we will soon be dealing with. First stop is the headquarters of *Operation Timothy* (the Christian organisation that is hosting us) where we are offered sandwiches. They are good sandwiches (though I would have enjoyed them less if I had known we would to billed for them later). There is barely enough time to settle in before we are bundled into a bus, then a train, then a bus, and taken to a German Colony hidden up in the mountains thirty miles away from the city. Colonia Tovar is an Alpine Village founded in 1843. Its white buildings and red tiled roofs nestle quietly into the hills amongst palm trees and strawberry fields. It is every traveller's dream. Diego and I spend the night in the home of a beautiful old German man in his eighties.

*Can it stop here? Can the clock pause? Can I sink my feet into these hills and eat the strawberries, until their juice runs red through my veins? Can I listen to the stories old people tell so slowly that history is lived all over again?*

The reason for our visit to the Pueblo is less than idyllic. We are going to an all-night-prayer-vigil. Most Latin American church services are too long for most Latinos; I am not with Latinos and it is not a normal church service. I know that once a Prayer Vigil starts – it will never end. There is no hope for us whatsoever.

*Please stop praying. Why are you crying out to God when you could be outside laughing, running, feeding your children strawberries? Kissing the golden dust of the earth in their hair?*

John and Jacqueline's fourteen-year-old son Rueben is the first to fade during the service. He becomes suddenly pale, the sight of his face reminding my morning sickness that it is the only one of us who does not mind what time of the day it is. After a brief foray to the bathroom, I do the only sensible thing that I can think of doing – I speak to the woman in change. Gloria is one of the founders of Operation Timothy and has organised much of the two-month outreach. The other important thing about Gloria is that she is the mother of Armando, the Director of YWAM Amsterdam. She is formidable. The more I talk with her the more I become aware of just how formidable she is. Maybe she has a softer more hospitable side to her like her son. If she does it is not a side that catches the light much. I suggest that the schedule would maybe need to be adjusted to make allowances for the children who are part of our team. I also point out that rest days are a YWAM policy, and I have not spotted many of them on the program. Gloria looks at me with the same look that God must have given Moses when he complains about the task ahead of him. She lowers her glasses and stares straight down the length of her nose, like she is aiming a crossbow,

"Have you come here for a holiday, or have you come to serve The Lord?"

*Doesn't Holiday mean holy day? Aren't all days holy?*

This is my second mistake. I was sent the program to look at whilst still in Amsterdam and had done little more than skim it, trusting that those who wrote it knew what they were doing. Problem is that I was not fully aware of Venezuela's political situation – it is not a place where you are supposed to trust people. Hugo Chavez has been in power for eight years. The Chavistas don't trust the opposition, the poor cannot trust the price of food from one day to the next, the middle-classes don't trust anyone. It is evident as soon as we leave the airport. The taxi drivers don't trust us to give them the right change, and if we trust them not to overcharge us, we are fools.

*I want us all to hold hands and look at each other until we become the same person. I want continents to stare across the water until they see how the contours of other countries used to hold them.*

A team meeting is called as soon as we are back in Caracas. Pouring over the schedule in detail we uncover a plan for us to go into the Amazon to spend time with a tribal group. There are impressive sounding meetings scheduled in churches all over Venezuela. Visiting missionaries are regarded as superhuman. It is well intentioned, but the pace is just too fast. Welfare of the group is priority.

*Should we close our eyes and trust no harm will come to*
*our children if we take them into the Amazon? Will God*
*protect the growing question of a child inside me?*

Gently, we ask if we can make some changes to the schedule.
"No." it is "all or nothing." It is a genuinely hard choice, but we
choose nothing. We are on our own in one of the world's most dangerous cities and are responsible for the diverse needs of a diverse
group of people. It is then that we are given the bill for the sandwiches.

A friend puts us in touch with a pastor whose congregation is in
one of the most dangerous areas imaginable – Propatria. You could
argue that things have gone from bad to worse – but we don't – we
are too tired.

The building huddles on the lower slopes of an infamous barrio.
Even the taxis will not venture up to the higher levels. They tell
us not to be out after nine. Abayomrunkoje, of course, leaves the
church regularly to wander the streets in his vest and gold chains.
He looks like a skinny Mr T from the A-Team, though he is not
such a team-player. Reasoning with him is impossible, especially
because he has been graced with the role of leader and is therefore
responsible only to himself. Aba wakes up in the small hours and
marches around the church wailing and chanting incantations. I
find out years later that he has the habit of drinking his first wee
every morning. Especially disturbing because there are only a few
cups in the church cupboard.

*Is this madness? Is the foolishness of Christ really wiser that human wisdom? Can I open my eyes and find it is just a strange dream?*

Another one of Aba's escapades is mentioned here:

*We go to Venezuela*
*With a prince from Nigeria,*
*A family from Australia,*
*Two pastors from Pakistan,*
*A crazy Croatian,*
*And a green haired Canadian.*

*It is here that I find out I am pregnant,*
*Where the air smells of petrol stoves and rotting mangos,*
*Where we are out-cast for our piercings and opinions,*
*Where I am sick morning and afternoon,*
*And organised religion turns sour, tastes bitter.*

*One day we go to a messianic church,*
*And sit in a row in front of a preacher,*
*Who tells us we will die early from eating pork.*
*As we are recovering from this information,*
*Our African friend grabs the microphone,*
*And prophesies that Carlos from the congregation*
*Will become the next president.*
*There is nothing I can do to stop him.*
*I feel sick.*
*And still do,*

*When I smell petrol or mangos*
*Or when I'm sitting voiceless, in a pew.*

I make an especially strong effort to erase the memory from my record. Though I do vaguely recall standing at the front of a church, microphone in hand, translating Aba's words into Spanish. Eyes widening as he corners an unexpecting member of the congregation, declaring loudly – and with all the finesse of a man drunk on the Holy Spirit – that the gentleman will be the next President of Venezuela. Maybe the country would be in a better place now if he had –Who knows.

*If Jesus could see this would he be laughing or crying?*

The poem also mentions problems caused by our appearance as a group. Some of us have facial piercings. I have dreadlocks. Venezuelan Christians do not know what to do with us, but they certainly know that we cannot be trusted. We are due to start working in a children's home, but they cancel last minute because "the timing isn't right for them". The real reason is because they do not like how we look. They tell this truth to the pastor, who tells another pastor, who talks to his sister, who writes it in an email to Armando, who tells us in person when he flies to Venezuela to sort out the mess with Operation Timothy, and with Abayomrunkoje. Armando has always been the only one that Aba will listen to. Though whatever Armando says does not work. If anything – Aba's behaviour seems to get even more unpredictable.

*How much did this trip cost? That little girl, the one who tells me she is tired of sleeping all in one room and listening to her parents have sex, how many flights would it have cost to buy them a bigger house?*

Diego is taking most of the strain because my *morning* sickness leaves me virtually incapacitated. I am throwing up more often than I am eating. Physically I am broken. Mentally I am exhausted. Spiritually I am being stretched. Thinner and thinner. Until one night, whilst trying desperately to sleep on that hard church floor, I snap. Not a snap audible to the group. It is a quiet snap that I feel internally. It is the snap of a guitar string tired of playing the same tune, it is the snap of an ant's knees giving in because it is trying to carry something too heavy, it is the snap of a lid going back on a pen after the writer has decided that a story just is not going to work. It is the snap of fingers instructing the words I am thinking and the words I am saying to become one and the same. I have given up on Christianity. I have had enough.

There are other things in Venezuela though, things I have not stopped loving. There are the kids who wander down from the Barrio to hang out with us outside the church. There is the strong faith and good attitudes of Gul and Kaleem. Men who work hard and never complain. Men who tell me that they respect the authority of my leadership, even though I am a woman more than ten years younger than them. Men who have been persecuted and shot at for their faith, and who still have not turned their backs on it. I have not given up on everything. I still care when we flatten a tiny rat-infested house to build a better one for a mother and her children. I still care about so much. I just no longer care to be part of a system designed to protect those on the inside from the beautiful broken world that comes carrying white flags, not weapons. I care enough to think about changing sides. I care enough to start to dream past the hardness of that church floor, and the vastness of its ceiling. I care enough to dream of a world where the stars are not hidden by walls.

Returning to Amsterdam does not help. I do not know what a missionary is anymore. We briefly try to join a small arts group. When I hear someone being told that, "It does not matter how they wave the ribbon, as long as they wave it for Jesus," I know that YWAM is no longer for me. By now I am heavily pregnant and still vomiting occasionally on public transport. I am trapped in a hinterland: no longer knowing how to be a missionary, or how to begin to exist in the real world. I am also about to become a mother.

# Home Birth

After so many years the decision to leave missions is equivalent to turning our back on our own family, and on the values and security that come with that. The YWAM leaders in Amsterdam are kind to us when we tell them we are leaving. This almost makes it harder – *are we making a mistake?* We leave in the autumn of 2006 and move into a small room in the beautiful town of Haarlem. The house is owned by a Dutchman called Ronald who has rented out all his rooms – including his own bedroom – and moved a mattress into the living room to maximise profits. Ours is an attic room, with a young French chef living only a thin partition away.

I feel like Mary riding the streets on a bicycle instead of a donkey, making the best preparations that I can in limited circumstances. Vulnerable, unsure of the future, in need of a community to hold me. A vacuum has been created by the subtraction of security, structures, and belief-systems. Oliver's arrival is a painful recalibration into humanity. It is a paradigm shift. The rebirthing of a translucent soul into a concrete world. It is a time when I stop seeing my neighbours as non-Christians waiting to be converted and start seeing them as fellow humans. I look at people and squint my eyes as the clouds between us lift – the lines separating *us* from *them* have evaporated, I do not know where I start and where they begin. I am made immeasurably bigger and immeasurably smaller by the experience.

Home-births are the norm in Holland. Someone comes to check that I can be lifted out of the window on a stretcher if there is an emergency, and we are good to go. We erect an alarm system – from our window to the ground floor using a bicycle bell and a piece of string – to let the midwife in without waking up the entire household. There is no point – my screaming wakes them anyway.

The following morning a blanket of the fabled peace depicted on Christmas nativity cards settles, blending with the smell of lavender from our broken oil burner. Our housemates come to visit bearing gifts. The first to arrive is a gentleman from Burundi. He gives us a gift of money, telling us that his tradition dictates that this is the correct way to greet a new baby. Our French neighbour drops by with pastries. The third visitor is a young man from the room beneath ours. We share a bathroom with him and can hear the constant sounds of his video games, but we have never met. "Play station six!" is his exclamation on entering. "Deep shit man. Deep shit," he shakes his head slowly from side to side. It is impossible to understand what any of this means until I stop seeing the world from my point of view and start seeing it from his – he is over-awed that this child of the future will witness computer games that he can only dream of. A baby means all things to all people.

Slowly, I am becoming aware that the miracle of life itself – laid bear with its legs kicking – means that a huge un-named monumental something will always remain. No matter how much of everything else is removed. No matter how many walls fall down – and walls are falling down all around us. Diego cannot find work, so we have to leave. I love Holland. I love the bicycles, the beautiful blunt directness of the people, I love the parks, the canals, the bridges. I love that people leave unwanted items outside their houses every time they redecorate (which is often). We amass a large collection of weird and wonderful things during our two years in the country. Now that we are leaving, these things are returned to the streets to wait for someone else to find them.

### Leaving Holland

*When we flee The Netherlands*
*We leave a pyre of possessions*
*On the corner of Overtonstraat.*
*We cut them loose like limbs*
*That take years to grow back.*
*An absurd flotsam of things,*
*Like baby teeth, thrown to the birds*
*On an urban beach:*

*A double loft bed with upturned legs,*
*A second-hand cat,*
*An orange beanbag –*
*The colour of the kingdom*
*That has no place for us.*
*We leave with a sleeping baby*
*And our last sticky dregs*
*Of Dutch courage in a suitcase.*

What ensues, is a return to the UK that makes me sympathetic to what a rocket might feel when re-entering the atmosphere. I am carrying a young baby and the weight of an increasingly depressed husband. I am trying to adapt to a culture that no longer understands me. We spend an awkward few months living with my parents. My mother decides that the best way to get us to go to church is to Vacuum outside our bedroom door early every Sunday morning – any pre-existing desire I might have had to go is sucked away into oblivion.

CHAPTER 9

# Motherhood

We move out when we can and go to live in the city of Derby because we have several YWAM friends who live there, and we need the safety net of the familiar. My time in Derby is hard. I find one church that meet in a studio at the bottom of someone's garden. It is a nice church, full of lovely people. But the problem with my time as a missionary is not just that I am scarred by all the weird and wonderful things that happened to me – the problem is that I have been spoiled by community living. The people I was living with became like family to me. No matter how involved I get with a church, or how close I get to my neighbours – I will never be able to recapture that intense sense of camaraderie. Diego and I roll slowly around our small terraced house like two tired beans on a plate.

Motherhood is a deeply isolating experience. Me and my baby against the world – everything a threat. My heart is suddenly as soft as my child's skin. There is no reprise, not a second of it. Leaving my sleeping child in a cot in the next room feels like leaving half my heart in Africa. Babywearing helps. He never needs to cry because his body language tells me what he needs before he knows himself. The real fight of motherhood is not taking care of your child – it is taking care of yourself. Trying not to lose yourself completely in stinking piles of insomnia-soaked nappies.

Our second son Tahiel is born during 2008. Tahiel is a Mapuche name (an indigenous people group native to the Andes), meaning sacred song. We do not want both of our children to have British sounding names, and a native name shows the respect I want to show to South America. We later do a DNA test and find that my children are a fifth native South American, which I think is something to be proud of.

I hope two children will water down my love – it of course intensifies beyond saturation point. Love has more surfaces to reflect off. It refracts off so many crazy angles that it makes me dizzy. The first time that Ty laughs it is at his brother – pure crystalline adoration – tiny giggles of light bouncing around our poorly furnished bedroom.

The light from their faces helps counter the dark face of my marriage – so dark, that some days I cannot find myself in the mirror. It is by muscle memory alone that I wash my face and brush my hair. I get fat too – eating so I will expand to fill the space I am in, to be heavy enough to feel that I am really here, when deep down I am sure that I am not. Eating to feel the pleasure of food on my lips. Eating to feign satisfaction. It is his depression not mine, but it is all so unclear. I am losing my marbles one marble at a time, and I spend all day looking for them – under the sofa, in the mouths of my children, in the great pans of lentil soup made to make our money stretch beyond breaking point.

Some days though – some days I turn to face myself in the mirror and together we turn to face the world. Some days I look everywhere for love and know that if it does not come from within me, it will not come from anywhere. On these days I step into my messy kitchen and close the door. I turn the music up loud and dance to all the love songs because I know they are for me. On these days I wash the dishes with tears of gratitude running down my face as I listen to the parables seeping into my heart through stories on the radio. Even though my Bible is firmly shut, and I have no desire to open it, the sensation of a creator's fingers caressing the world seems to be expressed through all the precious art artforms that surround me.

There is nothing mundane about the day to day task of motherhood – *mumdane* – like a Great Dane, but bigger and fiercer. It takes more strength than scaling a mountain, more endurance than a marathon. Magic ices over the giant lumpy cake of my inexplicable motherness. Like a blanket of snow turning an uneasy urban environment into a fairy-tale.

Oliver is the child that I always dreamed I would have – he is kind and considerate and a thinker of deep intelligent thoughts. Tahiel is the child that no one could make up even if they tried – he was born with his eyebrows raised in an expression of wry amusement and often says things that make me spit my tea out in disbelief. The pain of my marriage and the joy of my children sits at odds – like strangers eating from the same table. I love Diego as well as I know how, but my love is not enough because he came to me broken – broken like the doors he punches, like the printer he drops when I do not do what he asks, broken like the words that freeze and shatter when he puts a hand up in my face when I start to talk about myself, broken like the mirror he smashes whilst I cower under the bed clothes. Some days I can do nothing other than find shattered pieces of myself staring back at me from the bedroom floor. Some days my fingers bleed in solidarity with my heart as I try to pick myself up.

It is Maya Angelou[26] who picks me up off the floor that day with the mirror. *Still we rise*, she says, embodying the universal feminine spirit. When we look to our partners to complete us with their eyes and they are looking elsewhere – *Still we rise* – When our families look up to us to be strong and do not notice that we are in a thousand pieces on the floor – *Still we rise* – When we have asked for help with housework so many times that we know that our voice has simply been tuned out – *Still we rise* – When we want to cease micromanaging a household and scream at the top of our lungs that we used to fun – *Still we rise* – When our needs have been ignored for so long that we ourselves forget we have them – *Still we rise* – When the crippling guilt of our imperfection goes from numbness to complete paralysis – *Still we rise* – When every step we take into what has stopped feeling like our future is like a nail driven into the dream of who we thought we would be – *Still we rise* – When we know beyond doubt that we have been given more than anyone could or should ever handle – *Still we rise*.

When you rise up as part of this wave of counteroffensive love and feminine energy you are part of something so much bigger than yourself – this makes you stronger – or maybe gives you the strength to become more vulnerable. Vulnerability paints the giant wave as translucent and shimmering. Maybe it is the way the thin skin of water trembles in anticipation of storms to come. Maybe the whole picture is just so unbearably beautiful, that it hurts a little to be part of such a thing. Love is a big word – there is room in it for memories of brokenness – and space for that brokenness to heal. There is room in it for doubt too, but it is that doubt that makes our faith in love so very brave – and so very beautiful.

*I don't know what it feels like to be loved*
*But I know what it feels like to wake up in the middle of the night*
*And to reach for a hand that is folded in on itself*
*Like a child in the corner of a room*
*Needing so badly to appear alone*
*that they draw away from the warmth*

*I don't know what it feels like to be loved*
*But I know what it feels like to love*
*What it feels like to embrace every last ounce of my doubt*
*And to hold it tight as it kicks and shouts*
*Its face damp against my skin*
*A child who knows you can handle his moods*
*A child who knows you will wait*
*until his breathing*
*until his breathing*
*until his breathing*
*is easy.*

*I don't know what it feels like to be loved*
*But I know what it feels like to jump*
*Legs churning from a bridge*
*And to hope that the river will have enough grace to catch me*
*Enough grace to carry me downstream where I can take root*

*Where I can learn to have enough grace to grow into a child*
*Who is brave enough to want to know*
*What it feels like to be loved.*

These years in this marriage. I am so far from the surface. So far from being able to show the world who I really am. I am trapped somewhere behind the daily chores of domesticity. But I watch as the seasons continue to change through my window. I keep listening to the radio as I wash the dishes. Art and music and screenplays show me that there are people out there living authentic creative lives, people who are touching the surface of themselves – reaching out to towards the only place where others can find them. I want to do that. I want to be found. I do not want to feel trapped anymore.

Motherhood under the wrong conditions leaves you feeling cornered. Like your heart is walking around outside your body, and the grey looming concrete world is closing in on it. But all corners still have ninety degrees of possibility. Each time I pick myself up I believe less in the power of corners. Corners lose their power when you turn your back on them.

I feel cornered on my thirtieth birthday. Diego is not in the mood for celebrating, so I ride my bike out into the countryside to clear my head. I soon come to a lake and observe two men fishing with a rowing boat moored beside them. Then I do something that I force myself to do sometimes. I turn myself around from the comfort of that corner to face the terrifying fulness of the world in front of me. It is a private lake and the access is restricted so I have to shout from where I am standing.

"It's my birthday! Can I have a go in your boat?"

They are startled enough to agree before they give much thought to it.

It is lovely to be in the middle of a lake that I've only previously observed from a distance. It feels like I am participating in life rather than just observing it. Out here in the middle of everything – making ripples. This next decade is going to be different. I am going to be proactive. I am going to take a deep breath and tell the world what I want in a loud confident voice – even if I am shaking on the inside.

I decide to ignore the fact that I do not have the time or the energy for it and start studying for a literature degree with the Open University. I am amazed that my brain still works after all the cells lost after childbirth. I am amazed that there is a big world out there that can still be reached after my world has shrunk to the size of two small children. Sometimes the only dream that we have the strength to carry inside us is a very small one – but as soon as it is born, it calls other dreams to itself like a ringleader in a playground.

We move to a village south of Chesterfield in 2010. It is a very white-middle-class area. Oliver is probably the only child with native South American blood, born in The Netherlands to an Argentinian father with Chilean heritage, and a British mother who was born in North Wales. For a few years I make fewer and fewer attempts to attend church. I am not even sure if I believe in God. One day a lady from the village mentions that she attends an Anglican church in Chesterfield. I ask if I can accompany her one Sunday and she agrees. After the service, it is announced that the congregation will be gathering in fields nearby for a picnic. I tell the woman I am with that I will go, and she is beyond horrified. "How can you leave your husband and kids for so long?" she says. "You should not be putting your needs before theirs – It just isn't right." I am shocked and upset. This is one of the first times I've left the house without my children for years, and my confidence as a new mother is shaky. Is this the sort of welcome and care that I should expect from church? I go to the picnic anyway. It is there that I start talking to a wonderful curate called Ruth. It is Ruth who tells me about The Order of the Black Sheep.

CHAPTER 10

# The Order of the Black Sheep

I am a wild horse by this stage. I remember the confrontation with my youth leader all those years ago when she told me to run on the tracks. I remember the decades that I spent learning about what it means to be a Christian – and those few short moments that I spent putting those things into practice. I remember the people who spoke (what they thought was) the truth in anger, rather than in love. I am a horse who does not like people much anymore. I don't like myself much either. It is not just about the romance of running free in the hills rather than on a racecourse. I am undomesticated to the core, hurting, angry – and alone.

## Horses

*I am the daughter of Doolittle*
*born onto the back of Black Beauty*
*holding the reins of infant wisdom.*
*Do you want to fill my head with knowledge?*
*so there is be no space left*
*for what I already know?*
*Are children that much of a threat?*
*Is innocence so dangerous?*
*I lose it anyway*

*when my best friend leaves me*
*for a horse.*
*How I hated them*
*how I hate.*
*Until my soul rears up*
*white eyed and ready.*
*"You are a wild horse who needs to run on the tracks,"*
*my church leader tells me*
*in the same voice her pastor used*
*to break her into conformity*
*when she was sixteen.*
*It is the horses in Argentina that call me back to the wild*
*ridden by men who can't afford cars*
*who haven't stopped being boys*
*by daughters of the Pampa who don't have rich papás*
*bare-backed and broken out*
*faces to the wind.*
*Now the horse is the art that immortalises me mid leap*
*the metaphor that will*
*never again run on the*
*tracks.*

The Order of The Black Sheep[27] is a church for wild horses and dropouts like me. For years I watch the members of its community, waiting for them to try to make me believe something that I cannot, or be someone that I am not – it never happens. Very slowly and hesitantly, I start to draw closer.

I have found an open-hearted and open-minded Christian community right on my doorstep. The name makes it sound a little like a cult – as much as some of its members might enjoy the conspiracy – that is far from the truth. The Order of the Black Sheep is an expression of the Church of England's desire to remain relevant to the post-church generation. Everyone who attends has a different religious background, some have no previous church experience – all are welcome. The existence of such a place makes me think that maybe *God* – or whatever you might want to call the underlying and overarching mystery of everything – does exist. I have lost my faith in weaponised religion, but I have not stopped longing for community I can identify with. It is a miracle that I find the only sort of Church that I can stomach – and the only sort of Church that can stomach me.

My first experience with the Black Sheep is when I help them decorate their first meeting place for its inauguration by the Archbishop of Canterbury – Rowan Williams. Most of the walls are painted black. There is a Gothic dining room, an American diner, a church sanctuary decked out with black bean-bags, and toilet doors without signs on them to make the space as welcoming as possible. Unusual images are strewn around the walls: a picture of a UFO with the slogan *Do You Believe?* A sketch of a homeless man begging with the word *Change?* And a London tube emblem reading *Underground Services.* The most important feature of the building is a fully equipped kitchen. I have been to so many church services where we are lucky if we get a cup of tea and a biscuit at the end of the *meeting.* Here food and conversation seem to be at the centre of everything.

I take a photo of Rowan Williams in front of my mural in the gothic room (a painting of an old tree carved with an ancient poem in runes) – I am impressed that he can read it. As one of the chattier members of the group – I notice at one point that it has been left up to me to make small talk with him. I am not sure how one goes about making small talk with an Archbishop. I hear myself telling him that he will "know where to come if he needs a mural painting for St. Paul's Cathedral." He gives me that bemused look that people often give me. But later, when he is descending the stairs on his way out, he looks back up the stairwell towards me, points his finger and thumb in a jovial gesture, and says – "I'll be in touch". I am waiting for his call.

Mark Broomhead is my vicar. He has done lots of other things too, like being in a famous Heavy Metal band, and teaching home economics. One of his favourite things to do is to set up welfare tents at festivals to help care for anyone who is a little worse-for-ware. In my YWAM days this would have been a great opportunity to evangelise. Mark does not seem to have any desire for that. He gets on with things quietly and tends to avoid making too much noise – unless he is behind a guitar. Recently, when a homeless man from our neighbourhood died, he spent time quietly gathering members of the homeless community to ensure there would be people at his funeral. I would trade ten thousand hours in spirit-filled evangelical adrenaline pumped meetings for one service like that.

What I like best about our church is its authenticity. If I ask someone how they are I get an honest answer – which sometimes includes swearwords. Meetings are focused around questions and discussion, rather than answers. I am most definitely not saying it is perfect – far from it. We are a messed-up bunch, and I like that we do not try to hide the truth of that. I also like that church activities take up very little of my time. Religion had previously been so all-consuming that there was no space left for anything else. Now I am able to spend time as part of my local community. I am able to enjoy being with people outside the church. My soul can lean back – spreading out its arms on the soft leather of the ever-expanding giant sofa of friendship.

CHAPTER 11

*Friends*

I have made five friends in the supermarket, at least four in the park, and another through selling a chair on eBay. I made two wonderful friends in IKEA. The first was a woman I helped when she was struggling with her shopping; she sent me an orchid in the mail to say thank you. The other encounter happened when I started talking with a South African woman who was admiring my hat. We realised immediately that we loved each other and were soon hugging and catching up like long-lost friends; no one watching would guess that we only just met.

Recently, I sat near a beautiful Iranian woman on a train and she asked my advice on a big dilemma she was facing – five minutes into the conversation she asked if I would be her sister. I accepted of course. We are still in touch – the other day she visited for the first time and we talked and cried and poured our hearts out into the small hours. I need as many sisters as possible. In a society where we are told that we should fit seamlessly into a tidy box with 2.4 above average children and a perfect partner, we are starved of a sense of real community and we desperately need to find our tribe. Strangers are important because they are one of two things: someone you will never see again, or someone who will become part of your life.

There is a whole universe in a person – whole galaxies of stories that you might only have one chance to hear.

When I ask myself what it is that fuels these encounters, there are a few factors that come to mind. The first is an overpowering sense of curiosity – like a giant itch I want so badly to scratch that I lose all sense of dignity. I was at the cinema with some neighbours recently and there was a woman sitting at the back of the theatre who looked distinctly Latin American. I glanced back at her a few times during the film, wanting to know if I was right. When the film ended, she walked out of the theatre next to me and I found out that she was from Colombia. She visited with her husband two days later; we shared South American food and chatted until late in the evening.

The second factor is a lot harder to pin down. It is about how love is drawn to love, and open-heartedness is drawn to open-heartedness. While my curiosity is, at least partially, under my control, this other aspect seems to follow its own unique brand of physics. But eyes show a lot, don't they? If you judge a person negatively on your first encounter, she will know it instantly by the way you look at her. Conversely, absence of judgement is an open door into a conversation. Absence of judgement creates a vacuum that draws love towards it.

Maybe all these encounters are fuelled by the nuns – by the way that trip with them inspires me to be open to sudden changes in direction. To hold onto my route plan loosely. To keep my eyes peeled for drunken moments of wonder. Maybe those adventures in The Andes ruin me for the ordinary. Maybe they turn the ordinary into an adventure.

Maybe some of it deliberately steps beyond serendipity. Goals have always deceived me – my mind moves goalposts so easily. When I get the job, or the relationship that I always wanted, I am still left wanting. I do not know when it is that I decide that naming genuine healthy *connection* as one of life's goals allows these goalposts to expand and move forward naturally and comfortably.

There is one more thing: shifting theology seems to shift patterns in my life. Or maybe it is shifting patterns that shift my theology. I never know which comes first – I think it is both. A mystical view of God creates a relationship with the Divine that is fuelled more by curiosity than it is by answers. A mysterious God is a force I might be inspired to try to find in a person who is *other* to me – to encounter such a God I must adventure into the unknown. I must try to understand people I do not usually associate with. I must cross all sorts of frontiers if I am to continue my attempt to know more about the open-hearted creative God I am choosing to believe in. When I remove the theory of Penal Substitutionary Atonement, I am left with stories of a Jesus who spent his life reaching out past expected social circles to *the other* – to the woman at the well, to the centurion, to lepers, to tax collectors. It seems that it is part of the nature of the Christian God to do so. As I said at the beginning of this book: *The characteristics that we give that mind* (behind the universe) are the characteristics we choose for ourselves. *Permission to be both open-hearted and creative is given when we grant the same qualities to the architect of the universe which we then inhabit.*

Maybe this all helps explains some of the reasons why I have so many strange conversations with people. Maybe it explains none of it. Despite giving it plenty of thought, I still do not completely understand what is going on. I went through a phase of noting down conversations to see if I could spot a pattern:

### Stephen (a Chinese Canadian who I meet on a bridge in Oxford)

| | |
|---|---|
| *Emily:* | Are you from Oxford? |
| *Stephen:* | I'm Canadian. Where are you from? |
| *Emily:* | I'm British |
| *Stephen:* | You don't look British. |
| *Emily:* | I was born in Wales. People often think I'm foreign. Having a foreign surname doesn't help. |
| *Stephen:* | What is your surname? |
| *Emily:* | Garcés |
| *Stephen:* | That sounds Spanish. [singing] |
| | Volare, oh oh |
| | E cantare, oh oh oh oh |
| *Emily:* | It that your song? *[research tells me that it's a Dean Martin song[28] with some Italian lyrics]* |
| *Stephen:* | No, that's the most famous Spanish song in the world. You must know it? |
| *Emily:* | I think I've heard it. |
| *Stephen:* | Of course you have. |
| *Emily:* | What's your name? |
| *Stephen:* | My name's Stephen, and I want to ask you if you mind that I take your picture. |

*Emily:*     OK... What will you do with it?

*Stephen:*    (taking picture) Will you marry me?

*Emily:*     I'll think about it. Did you say that to get a smile?

*Stephen:*    I'm making a book, of my fiancés.

*Emily:*     A book of your fiancés! Right. This is what's going to happen now. I'm going to take a picture of you for my book of fiancés –

I still have the picture of Stephen, smiling in the sun on that old Oxford bridge. He is the only person in my book of fiancés. I wonder how many are in his. There are a lot of questions we could ask about Stephen.

*Ralph (I find Ralph lying drunk at a bus stop clutching a binbag)*

*Emily*:     What've you got in your bag?

*Ralph*:     Motorbike gear

*Emily*:     I'm guessing you've not come on the bike today then

*Ralph*:     I just bought the gear off the market. I got the bus from Derby. My missus bought the bike trousers and I wanted the jacket to match.

*Emily*:     Won't she be worried about you, your missus?

*Ralph*:     She died.

*Emily*:     She died? When did she die? So, she bought you the stuff for your bike before she passed away?

*Ralph*:       Yeah

*Emily:*       Was she ill?

*Ralph*:       Yeah, she was smoking and smoking. Me and me brother-in-law were telling her to stop smoking and she won't listen to me and she won't listen to him. And she died at me brother-in-law's house. She died with her mouth open.

*Emily*:       I'm sure a lot of people die with their mouths open. Have you been drinking more since she died?

*Ralph*:       I didn't drink before she died. Her name was Pamela. I'm on me own. I've got two cats. At night I keep on thinking she's there.

*Emily*:       You have a lot to deal with by yourself. Have you found any organisations that can help you?

*Ralph*:       I'm still hurting

*Emily*:       Of course you're still hurting. I don't know you, but I'm concerned for you. I don't want to see you on the floor there. I want you to be safe and warm. It's cold isn't it today. Pamela wouldn't want to see you like this would she? Especially if you want to be riding that bike.

*Ralph*:       It's not me what's got the bike. It's me brother-in-law's. He might give me a backie.

*Emily*:       Do you have other hobbies?

*Ralph*:       Just bikes. I've got books on bikes and models of bikes. My favourite bike is the Honda Goldwing. I'd like to get on the back of one. It's like a settee,

*Emily*:   Listen Ralph, if I find you on the floor there again,
           you'll be in trouble. You need to find a reason to stay
           out of trouble.

*Ralph*:   I'm looking for another partner.

*Emily*:   Well it's all internet dating these days.

*Ralph*:   I don't know how to do the internet. I'd like to get mar-
           ried again.

*Emily*:   Was that your wedding ring?

*Ralph*:   We were engaged. We met in school. We were together
           fifty years.

*Emily*:   This is your bus now Ralph. I checked the times for
           you, and you have to change at Alfreton. Take care of
           yourself now won't you.

One of the things that moves me the most about my conversation with Ralph is how it changed the attitude of the onlookers. As
I approached, I could see people standing back from him, trying
their best not to acknowledge his presence. As the conversation pro-
gressed, I observed how they started to look straight at him and to
relate to his humanity. Taking the time to listen to people's stories
stops us viewing them as if they are made of cardboard – a two-di-
mensional world is a depressing place to live in.

I never see Ralph again, but I sometimes wonder if he ever got
his ride on the back of that motorbike. I wish him all the Honda
Goldwings in the world.

Listening to stories is often the easiest way for us to get past the
mechanism that causes us to judge on appearance. But the more we

listen – the more we do not have to. We start to assume that the stories are there even before we start to dig them out. We stop seeing a seemingly ordinary individual with a good story as the exception to the rule – and we start to see them as the norm. There is not a single person without a story to tell. There is no ordinary. I have tested this theory. I test it at the checkout every time I go to the supermarket:

*Emily:*   I remember you. You're the one who has never tried hummus.

*Angela:*   I don't like the look of it. I don't like the colour.

*Emily:*   You don't want to try it because of the colour?

*Angela:*   Yeah

*Emily:*   Because of the fact it's beige?

*Angela:*   Yeah

*Emily:*   But so many foods are beige. Bread. Pasta.

*Angela:*   I can't eat pasta. Not with the sauce. I don't do wet and dry.

*Emily:*   You don't do wet and dry?!

*Angela:*   No

*Emily:*   So, what does that leave you with?

*Angela:*   Nothing. Not very much.

*Emily:*   Oh, I love you, you're so interesting. [pause] So how do you not mix wet and dry? So what do you eat? I have so many questions.

*Angela:*   I don't have gravy on things.

*Emily:*   You'd have soup though, because it's just wet?

*Angela*     No

*Emily:*     No, you wouldn't have soup?

*Angela:*    Because of the texture.

*Emily:*     So, what do you eat? Give me a typical day.

*Angela:*    Errr... Today I had bread with cheese, no butter.

*Emily:*     So that would be a meal?

*Angela:*    Yeah, so if I have a roast, I just have veg.

*Emily:*     You just have - the veg. So, you don't have the meat?

*Angela:*    No

*Emily:*     Are you vegetarian?

*Angela:*    Nope. I just don't like how it feels.

*Emily:*     But do you eat any meat? [pause] So you're not a vegetarian?

*Angela:*    No

*Emily:*     But you don't eat meat? If you don't eat meat, you're a vegetarian, aren't you?

*Angela:*    Yeah, I know, but. But vegetarians would look, wouldn't they, to see if anything is in anything- [laughs] -and I don't do that.

*Emily:*     I'm going to film a documentary about you. I'm going to come back with a camera, is that alright?

*Angela:*    Yeah, yeah.  [laughs] I'm weird.

*Emily:*     What do your kids eat?

*Angela:*    They like spag bol. I can't eat it though.  Can't eat tomatoes.

*Emily:*     Tomatoes are wet, then?

*Angela:*    Yeah and I can't eat onion cos they got wet on them.

*Emily:*     Just dry food then, but how do you swallow? [laughs]

*Angela:*    I just swallow, I'm fine.

*Emily:*     Do you drink a lot of water?

*Angela:*    Yeah, I drink loads of water.

*Emily:*     But, is that not like having wet and dry, to drink at the same time?

*Angela:*    No, I don't *eat* and drink.

*Emily:*     I need more time to talk, this is like, this is over so fast, I have so many more questions.

*Angela:*    Sounds like we're on a date! [laughs] Get yer coat.

*Emily:*     Yeah, it's a bit like speed dating…

I have shared some of these encounters with you to demonstrate the idea that adventure can be had close to home. All the best travel experiences involve interesting interactions between people. Cultural experiences do not only occur when one nationality meets another, they occur when one way of seeing meets another way of seeing, and these continents are colliding every day. Not everyone can afford to travel, but everyone can afford to span the frontier that separates one person's world from another's. The biggest regret is not for those who cannot travel, but for those who travel without leaving the hotel room of their own mind.

CHAPTER 12

# Travel

I never felt truly British – never felt that I quite fit in. Maybe it was my dark hair, the fact that I looked like a gypsy child, a foreigner amongst natives. Or maybe it was because of my untamed childhood spent between the sea and the mountains in rural North Wales. I have searched to regain that wildness since I left at the age of seven. Even before I visited my first foreign country, my heart belonged to the world. To the far reaches of it, to the unspoken languages, to the untold stories. My heart belonged to the other people who were reaching out in the same way. People oceans away. People who knew that belonging is more than geographical. People who wanted to belong to all of the places at once – and none of them at the same time.

Travel is a beautiful thing - but the reason you go is to come home. Home is a place – it is not a place – home is a place again. Maybe open-hearted travel is a form of enlightenment?

This poem is about the experience of going to those places that I held in my dreams as a child and about looking back from them with fresh perspective.

## Living the Dream

*I have drunk tea made from cocaine leaves in Bolivia*
*Hitched with drunken nuns across the border from Chile to Argentina*
*Stayed at the most dangerous place in Venezuela*
*With a prince from Nigeria who drank his first wee every morning*
*From a cup we all may have shared*
*I have driven with drug dealers in Uruguay*
*Lived with a Shining Path terrorist from Peru*
*Given birth in a shared house in Holland*
*Spent two homeless months dressed as a man*
*For a show at the Edinburgh Fringe*
*And the whole of the time in the back of my mind*
*I had this really crazy notion*
*I dreamt of the day that I would be able to have*
*My very own bedroom, toilet and kitchen*

I have always been interested in how we are dots on the surface of the earth, and yet carry the imprint of that world inside of us. As a teenager I sat at home longing to be part of the world's bigger picture, but when I went to all those places, I began to realise that I already was. There is an element of *the grass is always greener* to it. My conclusion is that *the grass is always green*. An ordinary life (complete with a bedroom, a toilet and a kitchen) should be a life that is desired and valued just as much as a life full of travel and adventure. So, although I am now travelling less than I used to, I am still living the dream.

# Creative Travel

Creativity is a word we associate primarily with the arts. A creative person is often thought of as someone who paints, or who plays an instrument. A definition of creativity could say that it *involves the use of the imagination or original ideas to create something*. I think that we are capable of being creative in all areas of our lives. This *something* that we are creating can also be an interaction between people or a travel experience. Once we realise that the only boxes around us are the ones we put ourselves in, we can be free from them. We can start to ask: *What can we do?* Rather than being limited to thinking: *What is usually done?*

This is the thinking that I apply in 2013 when trying to figure out how to get an affordable holiday for my family. I ask my internet friends if anyone knows of a holiday home that we can use in exchange for paintings of the local scenery. Two women get in touch, both of whom offer us the use of their second homes in Scotland.

A lack of funds can increase, rather than decrease possibilities for creative solutions. When we have money, we often choose the most obvious solution – which is not necessarily the best. When we don't have money, there is always something else we can give. Bartering is a great tool. In the past I have painted farm signs and received meat and eggs as payment, the flooring in my house was given in exchange for artwork, and my garden is fertilised with horse manure given in exchange for paintings.

# Scotland

The first week of our holiday is spent in a small cottage only meters from the sea front, in a village called Port William in Dumfries and Galloway. Travel for me will always be about people. Other cultures are fascinating, and people connect me to culture. The owner of the house tells me to look out for Frank and his shire horses and one day, when out walking with my boys, I stumble upon Frank as he is bringing one of his horses in from the field. Charlie is a beautiful working horse with a kind weathered face not unlike that of his owner. Frank is leading him with a simple blue rope wrapped gently around his neck.

I soon learn Frank's story. As a boy he had worked in the village's two hundred-year-old corn mill and had told his boss that he would buy it when he was older. His boss had scoffed, but many years later he did indeed become its owner. He shows me the place where his younger self made his claim to the property by scrawling the tiny words *Frank Gilmour Esquire* on one of the walls. Frank is living with his small family in a caravan near the water mill while it is being renovated. In the evenings when my kids have fallen asleep, exhausted after a day on the beach, I join Frank and his friend Stuart for cups of tea outside the caravan. We talk about his ambitious plans to restore the mill, and about the art of judging character and connecting with people. He tells me a story about a newly-widowed woman who dials his telephone number by mistake. The initial misdialled call leads to more phone conversations, and later to a visit to

Newcastle. You never know when these connections will appear, he says, but you have to embrace them when they do.

On one of these days I help Frank and Stuart build a replica Loch Ness Monster for them to float in the harbour during the village fete. We cut a giant head out of wood and I paint it in angry reds and blacks. The fact that I have come to Scotland with my paints means that I am ready for any inevitability, even this one.

After a week we travel a few hours north to our next holiday home in The Highlands: a tiny cottage that looks out across a misty sea loch. After spending a few days visiting tourist hotspots and eating ice-cream, I am dying to meet some of our new neighbours. If you own a second home and are only able to spend some of the year there, then I believe you are obliged to work extra hard at building community during that time. Many of the properties near the little house where I was raised in Wales have since become holiday homes; it is a battle to keep the heart in such communities.

One day I follow a sign across the street which advertises the sale of ceramic art. I am invited into the artist's home where we drink tea and chat for hours. She gives me some of her artwork and a CD recording of her local folklore tales. I give her some art materials that would be hard to come by in such a remote location. I am excited to meet her; I think that this is the connection that will add meaning to the second leg of our holiday. Then the next day I meet Cat.

She is cycling along the loch shore with her dogs running alongside. I notice her American accent when we exchange pleasantries and ask if she lives here or if she is visiting.

"Ach" she replies, revealing a hint of the German heritage in her American accent, "I live up over there overlooking the loch and the castle, but no one can ever find the house because I don't have a sign."

"I'll paint you a sign," I reply. "I'm here to paint some local scenes, so I have my paints with me." *Is it better to paint a sign rather than wait for one?*

There is a second's silence, but it seems like longer as I feel her size me up. Cat is a woman in her mid-fifties, she doesn't wear make-up, but doesn't need to because she has presence. You know those people who can look you straight in your face and see your soul. She does more than that. She looks at you like she is panning for gold; she shakes the whole of you up in her panning tray. The useless bits of you fall away shame-faced and the gold sits there exposed and sheepish.

"OK," she says. "There's some wood outside the house, and I leave the door unlocked when I'm at work." She looks me up and down once more, "You can paint me a sign".

The converted barn already has a sign outside it, words printed on a tin plate which read *No Stupid People Past this Point*. It is exactly the sort of thing I expect to find. I paint her a wooden house sign in olive greens and purples, complete with Scottish thistles. She loves it. We talk over a cup of tea in her kitchen later that week.

"What was it that brought you to Scotland?" I ask.

"My husband worked here as an Oceanographer."

"Is he Scottish or American?"

"He was American, but he died six months ago."

I don't ask for more details. Why should I? It is none of my business. Later in the conversation Cat starts to talk about how the property she owns in rural Oregon had recently flooded, and she talks of how someone she knew was scared of the cougars who roamed there.

"Here we complain every day about the weather," I say, "but luckily we have no weather or wild animals to be scared of."

"I've not told you how my husband died yet," she says.

At this point all manner of possibilities start to run through my head: was he harpooned by a charging stag or attacked by a rabid badger? I hardly dare to ask.

"He was struck by lightning," she says.

"Oh," I say, slightly relieved that it wasn't the badger.

Six months later Cat takes a trip to Oregon to move her house to a less flood prone part of her property (yes, they just pick up the house with a crane and move it, and it is not a small house). She asks us to dog-sit while she is away. Every day I walk Ben and Skye near the wooden bridge where her husband had been walking them when he died – they had found their own way home.

## Lightening

*I walk the dogs along the loch shore*
*in sight of the wooden bridge*
*where they saw their master die*
*the only witnesses*
*along with the curlews*
*and the whooping gulls*
*and the distant watchful sea eagle*

*today all is the same*
*as it was that day*
*just a tiny bit emptier*
*curlews cry for a second longer,*
*fishing boats hurry home a wee bit faster*
*and the dogs stare out to sea*
*with more understanding*
*than dogs should have*
*knowing all they love*
*could be gone*
*in a flash*

This moment of walking his dogs near that bridge is like a pebble that plunges right to the depths of my soul and lodges there. Other moments, if they are shaped exactly right, can skim across the surface causing joyous ripples that mark our souls like laughter lines. One day I take a trip to the small island of Lismore with my two young sons and our dog Eva. We walk for miles down one of the only roads in order to find the café where there is promise of cake. Exhausted after the endeavour, the walk back is too much for us. We hitch a lift to the ferry with a beautiful old bearded gentleman. His ancient little car is one he preserves only for use on the island. That car ride is photographed in my mind: the dog with her head out of the window; my boys with sand in their hair and chocolate cake on their T-shirts.

I return to explore further with my eldest son a few days later. This day is photographed with a poem:

## Lismore

*we ride to Lismore today*
*take a bike on a boat*
*down the whooshing hills*
*and up the ones that make me groan like a gruffalo*
*you, astride the cross-bar*
*on a cushion lashed with duct tape*
*laughing laughing laughing*
*and saying it is the best day ever*
*stopping at the only shop*
*for a whole tub of strawberry ice-cream*
*we eat it with a view of the island's sugar-sprinkled waters*

*when we go the wrong way*
*a sea-bleached woman fills our water bottle*
*sits us in her farm house kitchen*
*gives us a tray of Penguin bars*
*and homemade shortbread*
*tells us a tale of a local princess who is buried*
*without her pinkie*
*she can't remember what the story means*
*no matter*
*its sharing is enough*

*the last ferry is at eight*
*and I am sure that we'll be late*
*but we are early as the lambs*
*we sail past*

*whooping hellos and bye byes*
*we find one we think is dead*
*until its mother calls*
*and it runs to her on legs so new they hurt*

On hearing my stories, people often remark that interesting things like that don't often happen to them. I reply by saying that if you want an embrace from someone sometimes you have to be the first one to open your arms. My reason for embracing so many unusual situations is not because I want to turn my life into some sort of a weird pantomime – it is simply because I want to reach past the surface of everything. I want to really be on the sofa drinking a cup of tea if I am on a sofa drinking a cup of tea. I want to really be in the room with someone if I am in the room with someone. If I am cycling past a farmhouse I want to be inside the farmhouse. I want to really feel the ground under my feet when I am outdoors. I have always had a thing for wild swimming. In my opinion a view of a beautiful lake or river cannot be truly appreciated unless you make yourself part of it – unless you at least get your feet wet.

From Cat's house there is a view to the south of a small castle on a tiny island in the middle of the sea loch. It is beautiful to look at – but I want more. One evening when the tide is out, I wade out to it. I climb the steep steps that hug the castle wall and peer through a tiny window that I find at the top of them. I am rewarded by a view of a cluttered kitchen and a sink full of dirty dishes. Seeing the reality of the castle close-up does not destroy the romanticism, if anything it brings it closer to home – people who live in castles are ordinary.

To the west is another small island. This time too far out to swim to. Cat has a kayak next to the house – so I borrow it for the occasion. I paddle out to the island, and after exploring the ruins of another castle, I bump into a man on the beach who turns out to be the Dutch owner who had reportedly bought the island for a million pounds a few years before. He is very courteous, even though I have just invaded his island with a kayak.

The view from Cat's house looks different after these two experiences – I now know what it feels like to be part of the places I am looking at. It is the same with people and countries – we cannot pretend to understand them until we listen and engage enough to become part of their everyday lives. Until we become curious enough to care about all their details.

The last poem that I write on our holiday plunges even deeper into this feeling that the landscape provokes in me. I write it on a dark evening from the safety of the armchair that Cat's husband may have used. The song of the wind battling the waves comes in eerie verses through the cracks in the window frames.

## Listening to the Sea

*sew me a gown with more shades of blue, and I will wear it*
*write me a song that sighs and roars in the same breath, and I will sing it*
*compose me a waltz with more oscillations, and I will dance it*
*shine a light more alluring than the moon, and I will be drawn to it*
*give me a drink that quenches the soul and*
*not the body, and I will drink it*

*your metaphors are sand through fingers*
*you don't know what I feel like from the inside*
*you can only touch my skin, watch it shudder in the wind*
*so, let me give you goose-bumps*
*that grip your memory like barnacles*
*let the only thing you can hold on to*
*be the vastness of ignorance*
*for you will never understand*
*that I am sea*
*and you are land*

Am I writing about the sea, or about Scotland? Is it a poem about other people's lives or about my own soul? Is the poem trying to document my futile attempts to pin down the mystery of God in words? I leave Scotland newly aware that there is so much that I will never understand – and that there is so much that will never understand me. But my soul has drunk from the well of deep waters and I know that it will want more.

*America*

It is said that the word serendipity originates from the Persian fairy tale *The Three Princes of Serendip*[29]. These princes are described as *always making discoveries, by accidents and sagacity, of things which they were not in quest of.*

Serendipity is a wave you can ride. If you fall off the board, you can choose to either wade back to shore and sulk – or swim straight back to the deep waters and wait. If you wait you will never stop doubting that the waves will come, but you will have faith: doubt is a component of faith, certainty can be its enemy – and you can never be certain about serendipity. You cannot make a list of the things you are not in quest of. The pursuit of serendipity is internal rather than external – with practice it becomes part of who you are. There comes a point when you are no longer any more surprised by it than by the twitching of your own leg (I think that this is an odd example for me to use, when my leg twitches and surprises me. The subconscious is a strange place). When serendipity settles within you it soon begins to spread outwards: instead of your heart stopping when the world unveils its surprises – it is the world around you that is constantly surprised by your own unveiled heart.

My trip to Scotland makes me feel as if I have unleashed a thunder-ball of serendipity that is beginning to snowball. I forward the details of one of the cottages on to one friend who makes mosaic art with her beachcombings, and to another who is a painter of seascapes. Both can quench their thirst for the sea, and in return leave behind beautiful pieces of art to sit alongside my own. But what can I do next? What is the next big idea?

As I am pondering this, I receive an email from a fan of my artwork in Idaho.

Dear Emily—

A friend on FB shared a post that included a painting you had made–I think, "Cathedral of Trees"–and I clicked over and viewed your entire portfolio, here on this site. I was (and still am) utterly spellbound. I want to thank you for these glorious, moving, sacred-seeming images. I am curious to learn more about what it would cost to buy or commission a work from you.  But mostly, I just wanted to say, Thank You. And I guess, to ask you to thank the trees that inspired you, for me, would you? :) I mean, if there IS a way to thank them. I hope there is.  Oh! And! Something happened that I can't really ever remember happening before. You–your pictures–made me want so, so badly to PAINT. I suppose I'd have to learn how, first. But I just want to DO it.

Thank you, again!

Yours–

Heidi Juniper

———◇◇◇———

Oh Heidi,

You are a wonderful person.

I posted some photos recently with a few painting tips if you look for them. If you put the time in you will be able to produce something you are proud of. Plus, painting is good for you! I've come a long way in the last few years. Started painting when my kids were sleeping 7-12pm and that's how I got my working day in :)

Lovely to hear from you and would love to see some of the things you are going to paint.

Emily x

Dear Emily,

I've have SO much to tell you – and at the same time was so savouring the laziness of being on holiday - I found myself ravenous to do nothing - and thus I've put off replying to your email. It made me so happy to hear back from you, saying such encouraging and lovely things, and RIGHT AWAY. I hope this long email isn't an imposition on your time. I have difficulty in being concise. But please don't feel you are required to be wordy in return.

Thank you for saying I'm a wonderful person! I do work at being a kind person. It seems extra important to be adamantly kind whenever possible, online - anything else can be so easily misconstrued. And people can find harshness and rejection and criticism all on their own - most of us have an unpaid inner critic at the every-ready. All in all, it just seems so strange to me that the distance that the internet can create seems to give so many people a sense of permission to be unkind. Wha?

But I did have an extraordinary experience with your art - a sort of transcendent, beyond-self sort of thing - it was simple and obvious to just try to thank you. So: The night I found your art, I sat spellbound for the longest time - and the rest of the evening and all of the next day, I kept seeing paintings wherever I looked - out of the windows of my house, especially. And late the next night, I grabbed my husband (Paul) and asked if he would look at the art of this new artist I'd discovered... HE is the artist in the family - started drawing as a kid and got a gloriously useless bachelor's degree in it. Anyway, he pots and he paints, too - pottery is the main thing.

I'm not sure what to mention first. I showed him lots and lots of the paintings on your site - I remember saying, Oh! There's this one painting! I've BEEN there! And I found it and showed him ("River in Sunshine") and he laughed. Because—well—we live in Idaho, and I think you're in the UK? So obviously it's a different landscape. But also, I think the colours you used don't - at least not all of them, and in that combination - exist in that exact way in nature. But it had the exact FEELING of this place we went last year - on a hike - in the Sawtooths. It FELT like being in that so-special place.

So, Paul also loved your paintings. (I was super happy that we both felt rather strongly about the same artist.  Last time that happened was with, I think, Rothko. :D He tends to like... starker and more challenging things than I do.) I told him that your work had the biggest impact on me since I'd discovered Matisse - he said - he could see why.

And then he said something I found incredibly discouraging. (You'll see why in a sec.)  He said - you know - this person is just... on a level that is so far beyond most professional artists... She's just on a different plane... Something like that. And I'm not totally ignorant about art and technique and all that - but what I had noticed was how your art FELT. Your work puts me in a trance! And it had this appeal to me that made me want to do something like it. Not anywhere as accomplished, but - somehow - slightly similar - sort of? And then my sweet husband's accurate description of your ability woke me up and made me realize the obvious - that it would be really, terribly, awfully hard to paint like you do. Years and years of long practice and great effort. If ever, if at all.

So that was the discouraging thing. :D I can draw okay, I would say - I can draw to my own satisfaction. So, I am... I feel in over my head, thinking of trying my hand at colour. But you mentioned describing some techniques in some of your posts, I will look for those. Of course, the thing to do is just to TRY it - I'm working my way up to that. Luckily Paul has a bunch of paints – acrylics - I'm not sure. But I am thinking about colour. My fear is that I will aspire to beauty and what I attempt will just be outrageously silly and pathetic... But - on the bright side - it was IN-CREDIBLY encouraging and sweet to hear that you wanted to see what I would paint! I teach piano and I would feel the same towards anyone of any ability... So maybe how you feel is somehow like that. But still. It's immensely bolstering to have you say that.

Anyway... so, I've continued to see art wherever I look, on and off since I discovered your paintings. And today especially, the light was so lovely, and starting to fade - I grabbed a pencil and paper. Tried to do a landscape - been ages since I tried doing art of ANY kind - can't remember the last time I tackled landscape. Junior high? I think I had tried a few times & gave it up as impossible. Today, I was reasonably pleased with what I did. Fairly sure the tree at the center of my drawing defies physics. It's crying out for colour – we shall see. I'm gathering my courage. :)

Anyway, thank you so much for how you've changed my life! Genuinely. The world is so impossibly beautiful. You reminded me. And-sort of-gave me permission to take more time – look around – put a halt to things and see the transcendent paintings that are around me/ in me - that I would paint if I could. I didn't realize I had paintings in me, so to speak... It's an incredible joy to spend time with them and to see them in my mind's eye, even if I have a limited ability to put them into physical form. If I never can capture them - at all - I still feel - embiggened by the chance to at least SEE them.

I was thinking today - I've toyed with the idea of moving somewhere a little bigger - but our yard and neighborhood, I'm discovering, are so beautiful... It's going to take me years and YEARS to understand and internalize how beautiful. We can't move! Not yet!

Thank you!

For everything! And for writing to me!

(I said to my husband - I mean - can you IMAGINE?! If you discovered Matisse - and the very next day - she wrote to you?!)

Yours,

Heidi

———◇◇———

Heidi,

Can I come and live with you?

I have never been to the US and would really like to visit. If you did decide that you wanted any paintings or any artistic tutoring I really could come and visit for a week or two. If you helped pay for the flight, I could paint you as many paintings as you wanted.

I know this is a crazy idea, but I think we both might be slightly crazy, so hey:) A few weeks ago I posted some paintings to the US and paid a lot for postage – altogether it came to the price of a flight, and there was a part of me that thought that maybe it would've been more efficient to ship the artist instead of the paintings!

Please ignore me if my craziness is too much and I won't be offended.

Emily

And this – ladies and gentlemen – is how the plan starts to come together.

I tell Heidi that I won't need the full tourist treatment. That I will be content just to be in America. That I want to see what is on their TV and in their fridge. She tells me that her husband laughed at the idea of being the object of someone's anthropological quest to live inside an average American household – but that is exactly what I want: to experience America from the inside out, to stay awake all night and listen to her breathe when everyone else is sleeping – creepy as that sounds.

Slowly the plan starts to grow. I am invited to a Quel's wedding in Portland, Oregon at the beginning of September 2015, so I buy flights. Then I start talking to a woman in Kansas City and we decide to have her fly me out there from Portland in exchange for art classes. Heidi will pay for flights from Portland to Idaho. Then, bizarrely, Cat (my friend from Scotland) schedules her move back to Oregon for four days before my flight. *Who is creating these coincidences?* When I was a missionary in Argentina a visiting speaker prayed for me and gave me a word from The Lord: *God has called you to the east coast of America to preach against liberalism.* Fifteen years later I am being summoned to the left coast – I wonder if God suddenly had a change of heart regarding liberals.

The connections I make with people don't always occur naturally – sometimes I fabricate them. I start fabricating connections a week before I get on the plane to Oregon. I do it using Reddit. Reddit is a place on the internet used by some very interesting and uniquely intelligent people. I go to the area reserved for people from Portland and I post this message:

I am about to travel to Portland, Oregon. Does anyone want me to bring them something from the UK? I am filling my suitcase with marmite and tea… Is there anything else I should bring you?

These are the replies I receive:

1. Healthcare
2. The BBC. All of it. On DVD please.
3. I want the Queen Mum. Please try and not crease her too badly when folding into your laundry.
4. A hot British bloke
5. Holy shit I will buy you beer for Lucozade
6. A couple of cans of spotted dick pudding
7. Let's talk beer! I'd love a beer from Wales, and any Irish beer you can get your hands on that isn't distributed to the United States (O'Hara's, Guinness, Murphy's, Magners). I'm not sure what you need from Oregon in return, but I've been known to locate things from time to time.
8. Boris Johnson
9. I will very happily take you out for a pint of something Portland-y if there's any way you could bring me some Doom Bar. Safe travels!!
10. Twiglets
11. Clotted Cream! I've only ever had the stuff in the jars, and some that I made. I don't think it would make the trip but would love to try the real thing.

12. What's the biggest container of Marmite that's sold there?

13. A bottle of brown sauce would rock my world, actually.

14. A small antique from a local antique store. Maybe a small vase, ceramic jar, antique picture frame?

15. I'm surprised no one has asked for chocolate. Real Cadbury's chocolate. Not that Hershey's crap made here and sold under the Cadbury brand.

16. If you're willing to risk bringing back Kinder Eggs, I am willing to pay you 2x their value :)

17. Nutella. I want to have a taste test.

18. Minstrels please.

19. David Attenborough

20. Ribena! It is so expensive here. Have you left yet?

21. Mushy peas in tins, HP sauce, and pickled onions thank you thank you. I lived in Huddersfield for a couple of years and sigh.

22. Shetland Wool

23. Bounty bars. A case of Bounty bars. All of them.

24. Cadbury Flake, please! I want to better understand the series of 80s adverts...

25. A Tottenham Hotspur Scarf

My suitcase quickly becomes so heavy that I can barely lift it. I have to drink a beer and give a bottle of Lucozade to some teenage delinquents, who are playing on luggage trolleys, just to get it up onto the scales at the airport. My flight goes exactly as expected. I befriend a man called Rocky Blakewood as we are waiting to board. He is wearing blue jeans and a cowboy hat, works for

Daimler trucks and plays the hurdy-gurdy. We agree to meet up in Portland.

I am then assigned a seat next to a lady who makes me cry – I mean real tears, and probably a few shoulder heaves. There is no way out because it is a window seat. She is a Christian and this is a point in my life when meeting Evangelical Christians has a strange effect on me. All my post-religious questions and doubts and regrets have slowly settled down in the years since I have ceased to be a missionary. They are even covered with a thin sheet of dust. They only raise their heads occasionally as they reposition themselves, then the dust resettles. This woman rattles them, and they do not like it – well – they are not sure if they like it or not. She has noticed them at least, that counts for something. However, they are slightly ill-humoured after such a long sleep and may have said a few things they regret. I am almost certain that they apologise afterwards.

I arrive two days before the wedding and am picked up at the airport by Emily who is a friend of the bride; she will host me for my first few days in America. She recognises me by my yellow back-pack – I recognise her by the sign she is holding with my name on it. She seems confused to observe me awkwardly trying to give my details to a middle-aged man in a cowboy hat whilst being caught tight in a tearful embrace with my Christian travelling companion. My journey has started exactly as it is to continue.

It is evening as we drive back to her little wooden house. They are all wooden – all of them – and there aren't two of them the same. I love America already. I sleep with a whirring in my head, like springs are slowly coiling back ready to launch me into a month of limitless adventure.

When I awake it is like I have stepped into wonderland, or gone to Oz. I eat toast spread with magical jams harvested from Emily's garden and step out into the world. I look like a poster child for a mental institution – head swivelling constantly from side to side to take it all in as I walk: mail boxes and licence plates and porches and vegetables growing anywhere there is an empty plot of land. The first person to greet me is a transgender lady whose smile makes the mild September morning feel even warmer. I have never been one for cities, but if I did become one, I am beginning to feel that Portland is the one that I would become one for.

I'll never forget how I feel walking out of the house on that first morning. It is like stepping into a new identity, like starting to watch a month-long movie of which I am the protagonist. It can be a good thing to put your actual life on hold from time to time. I have been married for ten years and a mother for nine of them – and have almost completely forgotten who I am as a person and what it is that I want from life. I have been living as an extra in my own life. I have forgotten that it is possible to live as a protagonist, whilst still acknowledging that the extras in my life have their own shows in which each of them plays the title role.

It is very easy to believe this as I walk down Hawthorne Boulevard. Hippies and Hipsters sit outside quirky food vans talking politics over organic coffee and raw kombucha tea. Everyone in Portland deserves their own TV show. I will never forget meeting Kevin. He is sitting on his porch in his owl onesie, looking like the most relaxed person I have ever seen. Maybe he is high; it is only about a week before the legalisation of cannabis in Oregon. If Portland were to have a face – it would be his: sitting there in his rocker, hood of the comfortable blue and yellow owl costume framing the stubble around his slowly forming smile. I think that there is a part of all of us that wants to be a little more like Kevin. He shifts his position almost imperceptibly and points with an eyebrow to ask me if I want a pear from his pear tree. I take one, and that is the last I see of him.

I carry on walking and venture into a boutique selling old type-writers remodelled into coffee tables, and signs sporting the city's slogan of *Keep Portland Weird*. A woman is holding a pair of pink fox earrings up to her face and looking to her friend for approval. The friend looks at her earnestly and says "Yeah. Foxes are the new owls." I make a mental note to keep my ears open; there is so much Portland can teach me about the world. Rifling through some trinkets I fall in love with a ring made out of a silver buffalo nickel. The price tag says $40, but I urge the shop owner to call up the woman who has made it and we make a deal to swap it for a silver ring that I am wearing. This is great as I have not exactly budgeted for spending money. Well, I haven't exactly budgeted at all. I am just flying on the same stupid faith that I exercised during my more naïve missionary days. It seems that this sort of faith is not exclusively for the use of practising believers; it is starting to feel more like an actual scientific force that can be accessed by anyone.

It takes the full forty block walk into downtown Portland for me to begin to stop swivelling my head around quite as maniacally. I am not sure quite why this is. I have always felt that all of life should be taken in at once, and I have always tried not to miss any of its details. I was the sort of child who could spot a tiny beetle from metres away – before quickly becoming very best friends with it. Such

an intense level of observation and hypervigilance is probably why
I am an artist. It is also an exhausting habit. I cross the Hawthorne
bridge, one of ten which spans the Willamette River, eat an insanely
good burger and take the bus back to the house. My feet are tired,
but it is worth it to have observed – that yes – the whole city is indeed full of people who are crazier than me. I am vindicated by this
news. I am freer than I have ever been.

The evening finds me sitting on the porch with a large bag full
of HP sauce, beer, antiques and tins of mushy peas, as I wait for a
man who I have met on the Internet to drive me to The BeerMongers on Division St. I think his real name is Colin. His name on
Reddit is something that connects words and numbers in a way that
is deeply witty and impossible for a techno-novice like me to understand. I can usually tell if someone is trustworthy by looking them
briefly in the eyes. This kept me safe during my five years in South
America. Well, either that or I am just very lucky. Colin does have a
slight squint, like he has not seen daylight in a while, though his eyes
do have a glint of that deep humour predominant with Reddit users
– humour so deep it is almost buried alive. The bar is only a short
ride away. There are two girls already there when we arrive. We introduce ourselves, and they ask for Colin's Reddit name. They look
disgusted when he tells them and avoid eye contact with him for the
rest of the evening. Colin has been the instigator of a thread about
how a capybara had died a lonely death on a pile of ladies' bras in
an apartment he rented out in Portland. It is a long story apparently,
so I never get all the details – which is quite a relief.

The two girls each have a story of their own. The first has come
to collect some marmite and prawn cocktail crisps for her English

boyfriend who left the UK at the age of fifteen. He is having a bad week and she is planning to surprise him. The second girl has come for a Cornish beer called Doom Bar. The memory of it is tied inextricably to recollections of her treasured time in the UK. She has searched for it everywhere, but to no avail. I think that with time, Doom Bar obtained the status of the holy grail in her mind. She cries when I give it her. Actual real tears, which magnify her already big eyes, before adding to the beer stains on the floor. She gives me a scrap of paper with her phone number next to the words SAD DOOM BAR GIRL and invites me out for lunch, "I'll do anything for you. Anything," she says.

The beer is flowing. The barman is intrigued by our arrangement. He agrees to let us do taste tests with British verses American beers. Guinness for example seems to be a beer that doesn't travel very well, though it is hard to be sure of slight nuances in taste because of the amount of beer that I am consuming in exchange for the chocolate and tins of mushy peas that I am continuing to hand out. Oh, what beer! I think I try sour beer, pumpkin beer, porters that blow Guinness out of the water, and countless deliciously hoppy IPAs. I am a newly converted comrade in the American brewing revolution. It is a life changing moment. I can barely remember what it was like to live in a world without such a vast array of good beer.

I am not sure if it is a beer induced haze or if there is something ever-so-slightly holographic about the next gentleman to enter the bar. He tells me quietly that he is here for a large bar of Dairy Milk. I hand it him and he asks if I want the Star Wars or the Harry Potter Lego pieces in return (My kids have let me go to the USA on the condition that I bring them back a suitcase full of gifts). I choose the Harry Potter and ask him if I am depriving his children of their toys. "No," he says quickly. "They're all mine." Then he backs slowly out of the dimly lit bar and returns to the even darker and less demanding realm of the internet. Meeting people from Reddit in real life is a truly fascinating experience.

John and Karen are here too. I painted a portrait of their late dog Owen a few months back and they turn up to meet me in person and give me a bottle of wine. Out of all the people I meet on my trip John and Karen are perhaps those with the greatest presence. Not a presence that demands your attention, but one that just sits quietly illuminating everything around it. They have decided not to have kids and John has given up his job to focus more on charity work. He is the sort of atheist who gives atheism a really good name. Sometimes being near people for a few minutes can teach you as much as reading several of their books. Sometimes I look at people and I see libraries. I am glad I have a chance to read more as they are both keen to help me make the most of my time in Portland. Phone numbers are swapped.

I am driven back to my residence in a Mini convertible by a couple to whom I gave some plates decorated with English country scenes and portraits of the royal family. They tell me that the evening – although highly unusual – has been an immense success, and that they found prawn cocktail crisps strangely enjoyable. I tell them that I love them. It isn't the beer. I really do love them. It is a shame to be ruled by cynicism when it comes to love. I think people tend to forget how many kinds of love exist outside the box of romance. I am determined to use my American adventure to discover as many as possible.

When I get back to the house it is very late, and I am very drunk. It is not a state in which one is easily surprised, and the evening that I had makes me suspect that Portland's possibilities for surprise are infinite. I have somehow fallen into a perpetual state of knowing that someone is about to throw me a surprise party or leap out from behind a bush. As I collapse onto my bed, a message pops up on my phone from my Kiwi pilot friend Nathan, who I know from one of my previous lives in Amsterdam and Venezuela. I last saw him about a year previously when he visited us in England with his wife Leona. I had not expected to see them again for a very long time, but here they are in Portland at the same time as me without us having planned it – and we both have free time the following day. Wonderful. We will be able to surf the waves of serendipity together.

Nathan and Leona pick me up the following morning. We spend the day tasting the city's culinary delights: basil and lemongrass donuts, surprise trays of savoury goodness from quirky food carts, and coffee – really good coffee. We go into one coffee shop where the beautiful young barista is preparing drip coffee. As she eyes the slowly filling conical flask, I eye her tattoo. It is of an avocado. It does not surprise me in the slightest. In my eyes she is the perfect woman. She has most likely given up a well-paid and slightly stressful office job in order to serve coffee. I imagine that this gives her time to grow her own produce and cook most of it from scratch. The simple design of the tattoo, an egg-shaped line for the outer shape of the avocado and a small oval for the inner stone, gives form to the purity of her existence. The girl with the avocado tattoo is filed away in my mind together with Kevin in his owl onesie. If they ever meet, they will make beautiful babies.

Out of all the people from Portland who inspire me, none do so more monumentally than the woman I am about to meet next. Her name is Kiki and we meet her in a taxidermy shop on Mississippi Avenue. She asks if we are all travelling together.

"No, we just happened to be in the same city at the same time."

"Ah, that'll be the squirrels," she responds without pausing.

"Squirrels?!" I say, "I've tried religion, and philosophy and everything between – and the thing that makes sense of it all is *squirrels?!* Why has no one told me about this sooner? Do you have a book I can read? Can I follow you around for a bit?"

I write a poem to try to make sense of the conversation.

## My New Guru

*Under a hippopotamus head*
*In a taxidermy shop on Mississippi Avenue*
*A lady called Kiki from Idaho*
*Tells me that all the strange serendipity*
*And coincidences*
*And monumental instances*
*Are caused and planned and calculated*
*By the squirrels who live in my head.*
*The squirrels who live in my head?*
*You just put it better than I ever heard it said.*
*We laugh and I ask if she will be my guru*
*And we take a photo together*
*With some old friends from New Zealand*

*Who I have just bumped into.*

*Looking at it later*
*I noticed a stuffed squirrel in the background*
*Its glass eyes wide*
*And watchful*

For the rest of my trip it seems that every time I turn my head, I see the shadow of a squirrel flitting just out of my vision. I never get to understand their logic, or to ask one what the hell it thinks it is doing, but I become aware of their existence, and I begin to make allowances for them.

It is the day of Quel and Tristan's wedding. Nathan and Leona drop me off outside and drive off in pursuit of squirrels of their own. It is a beautiful little outdoor venue in the hills on the outskirts of Portland. The idea of an outdoor wedding is insanely magical to me. Portland is supposed to be one of the rainiest cities in the United States, but it is still possible to plan an outdoor wedding in September. Trees. Fairy-lights. Dresses. The downside is the fact that the Groom has just been diagnosed with Cancer. The fragility of love and life are palpable. Every word is poignant, every glance meaningful.

This is the very same Quel from my Christmas camping trip in the shadow of the volcano ten years previously. We went through a lot together during the time I spent as a missionary in Argentina in my early twenties. She was my saviour: a life-raft of logic and reason in a sea of fundamentalism. Flying to Oregon for her wedding is the least I can do to say thank you. I am excited to write one more story with her; we already wrote so many: hitchhiking with drunken nuns when we were stranded on the wrong side of a lake in the Andes, living in a warehouse full of aspiring artists in downtown Buenos Aires – clinging always to our buoyant doubts in the ocean of certainty that threatened to drown us. I love her in the way that a fellow soldier is loved when the war is over. The understanding between us is deep.

I know many of the guests from my time in South America. It is wonderful to see them again, though slightly unsettling – they remind me of who I was before. There is a huge amount of catching up to be done, which is why what happens next is surprising: I start talking to a woman called Andrea who I have never met. She is tall, slim and beautiful with very short dark hair. There is a depth and a humour to her that is magnetic. I know that this woman will be an important person in my life. We talk about everything, including our failing marriages. It is easy to be extremely candid with a stranger: the best sort of therapy – and the cheapest. She tells me she lives in Corvallis. "Oh," I say, "That's where I am going next. I met a woman in Scotland who just moved back there." Andrea tells me that I can go and stay with her first. So, I do.

It is my second time inside an American household, and my anthropological study disappoints me yet again. It is not like the TV. There are no donuts, only hummus and cucumbers. I have to keep remembering that this is Oregon, not America. On my second day with Andrea I am introduced to two people who still eat hamburgers – an elderly lesbian couple, desperately trying to hold onto their deep-rooted deep-fried culinary traditions in a neighbourhood that is quickly being taken over by expanding wholefood co-ops and

young liberal families with front yards bursting with organic produce.

Andrea talks to me about all sorts of things. Our conversation
gets very deep very quickly. I start to realise that she is the American version of me. We are both approaching the end of our re-
spective marriages and we stand together to face the beginning of
something new. Andrea and I now speak and message almost daily.
We have grown together like two new souls, sharing mistakes and
heartbreak. We post care packages to pick each other up when we
fall down. We hold each other up across the ocean. Maybe it is an
*imprint* thing like with baby geese. Maybe we are two new souls
who latch onto each other at that moment of birth – because if
divorce is not a born-again experience, then I do not know what
is. This life-long friendship is birthed in just two days. We open up
and connect; our souls graft together. We share things that we have
never shared with anyone. This is a pattern that will continue with
the people I meet for the rest of my trip. Wonderful insight can be
gained through a visiting outside perspective. Secrets can be shared
and carried away to safety.

Cat picks me up the next morning and drives me to her big
property in an area called Soup Creek, out in the wilds on the edge
of Corvallis. The light floods the grasslands surrounding the house
as if in memory of how the creek had flooded the house a year earlier. It is a landscape frequented by coyotes and the occasional cou-
gar. We hike out through the poison oak infested woodlands that
night to borrow a phone charger from one of Cat's neighbours who
lives in a giant wood cabin on stilts the height of trees. On the way
back, I realise that she is only using the flashlight for my benefit. We

are both actually more comfortable walking in complete darkness. I have always disliked how the small circle of bright light around your feet prevents your eyes from being able to adjust to anything that might be happening slightly further away. Walking at night is magical. The concept of distance is completely removed – you become part of the bigness of everything. It takes me back to how it felt walking to neighbour's houses in the Welsh foothills with my mum. We would navigate the country lanes using only starlight. If it was a long walk, we would chant the incantation *hot chocolate, drinking chocolate, hot chocolate, drinking chocolate* to summon the thought of the nearness and warmth of home.

Cat chats as we walk. She tells me about her neighbours, painting such colourful characterisations that I begin to feel that the landscape has sucked me into a novel created for my benefit. She speaks of Hank who has hoarded wood in his woodshed for decades, whilst never seeming to use it. When a neighbour asks to borrow some, he always says no. Maybe he will build an arc if the creek floods again. She tells me how the neighbours jokingly referred to her house as *Flamingo Acres* because of the lawn flamingo positioned by her mail box. I offer to paint her a sign to make it official, and to complete the symmetry of how we met in Scotland. Imagine meeting a woman as she is walking her dogs and then spending the next day painting her a house sign, then being asked back to look after her house and dogs whilst she is away, then accidentally following her and the dogs to America, where you paint her another sign and help her unpack.

It is wonderful to see the dogs again. The shaggy grey collie, Ben (named after the Scottish mountain Ben Nevis) insists on sleeping in my room for each of the four nights that I stay here. Cat explains this by saying that he doesn't trust her; Ben still wonders if she is responsible for his master's death, even though he was there when it happened. The logistics of being struck by lightning are not an easy thing to explain to a dog, especially a sheep dog like Ben who does not listen well and is easily distracted by the possibility of someone throwing him a stick, or the sound of an approaching car that he can chase.

I receive an unusual message on my second day in Cat's house. It is from a fan of my artwork who is amazed to learn that not only am I in the United States, but I am only an hour away from them. Randy wants to arrange an art class for his wife Bee, to help her regain some lost confidence. They arrive the following morning and drive me into Corvallis for breakfast. Randy is a Vietnam veteran who is as big and as warm as Father Christmas, with a beard and deep set twinkly eyes to match. Bee is soft and motherly, with an expressive face set exactly halfway between worry and love. We eat breakfast burritos in a bakery, drink more good coffee, and finish it off with tiramisu. The combination of food and company is like heaven. Whilst I eat, I tell them everything I know about art. This is as formal as the class gets.

As the conversation flows, I begin to piece together Bee's story. An illness had forced her to take a redundancy from her work and she had started art lessons to alleviate stress and boredom. The art teacher had been of little use. At one point he criticised her work and screwed it up in front of her. His attention reserved instead for a young blonde with large breasts, who paints ridiculous abstract pieces and receives nothing but praise. Bee turned to art to boost her confidence and the opposite has occurred. I give her a pep talk that goes something like this:

*Art is not a safe space; it is a brave space. You go out on a limb, and someone cuts the branch. It hurts, but it does not mean you should stop climbing. I hope new words will silence the echoes of old words. Listen for a while until you can hear the word "painting" without hearing the word "pain".*

*Talent is overrated and used as an excuse. It reduces someone else's skill set to fairy dust. A cloud of it surrounds them and makes everything they do effortless. Believing this about them makes what they have feel unobtainable. People get good at things because they spend a lot of time learning how to do them, not because they are naturally gifted. Put in the time. Paint into the small hours and wake up with it in your hair and behind your fingernails. Fight to improve and you will.*

*There are shortcuts. Millions of them. No one gave me shortcuts. I went the long way around and made a lot of wrong turns. I did not know how to think in layers. I didn't know what paint is capable of. I didn't have a relationship with it. I tried to tell it what to do, without listening to what it wanted.*

*Understanding the nature of acrylics is like understanding the nature of God. Both are immensely forgiving, and it takes forever to know entirely what they are capable of. Trust the acrylics, and mistakes can end up enhancing – rather than ruining – the painting. If you have to re-start your initial sketch you haven't wasted time.*

*That time has been spent looking, thinking, and observing – these things are more important that the act of painting itself. If you get somewhere on your first attempt, it is not usually as good as the place you could get to on your second or third or fourth attempt. True insight is not instant. We have to look at something over and over and over again before we can see it for the first time. Paintings gain depth from imperfection. Perfection is an illusion, it is nothing but a mirage, a way to keep us moving forward. Paintings are our life stories: full of false starts, dead ends, weak boundary lines, misplaced certainty, unnecessary caution, excessive inhibition.*

*Like the old proverb, I can give you all the techniques I know, or I can give you the means to find your own techniques. Curiosity is the best thing for that. Curiosity is the knowledge that there is a tree growing in front of you full of delicious, impossible fruit. Fruit that is free for the picking. Fruit that will taste and look completely different, depending on the season or the time of day. Everything is there: subject matter, texture, lines, movement, time, space, community, memories, life, death, colours that sound like music...*

*The main thing to remember is that you will get out what you put in. If you use art only as a deposit for your pain, then that is what you will find there. That is what you will hang on your wall. If your art is completely devoid of emotion your canvas will be blank no matter what you put on it. If your art pretends to be something that you are not, then the paint will probably flake off after a few years. But if you paint what you want to feel (even when you do not feel it) and what you want to see (even when you do not see it), then that is not a lie about the present – it is just the truth about the future.*

*If you feel that your creativity is limited by such things as time and money, then please understand that such limits increase rather than decrease creativity. If you have too much money for materials, you will never be forced to be inventive with what you have at hand. The possibilities would be too overwhelming. There would be no starting point. If your time is unlimited you would probably start a painting and never finish it. Or even worse, never start at all. Time that is limited forces you to attack the moment like a child.*

*Let your limitations be your springboard: create sculptures out of coat hangers, make collages out of sweet wrappers, use materials from a DIY store instead of an expensive art supplier, paint with tooth brushes, with kitchen sponges, with your fingers. Paint only with the power of your mind. Try new things until you find something completely original – something you are the first to try, something only you can do.*

*Art is nothing more than an expression of your existence. You do not exist any less than anyone else does – why should your art be worth any less? Paint. Go to sleep with it on your mind. Wake up with it in your hair. Work with it between your fingers. Fill you house with it. Write with it. Sing with it. Dance with it. Cook with it. Play with it. Dream with it. Paint.*

I wave my arms around a lot and spill my coffee a few times in the process of delivering this monologue. It takes courage for some-one to make those first few marks on a canvas. I will happily attack anyone who deliberately discourages them. It is a thing I am pas-sionate about – angry even. Artistic souls need love.

I then write Bee a more detailed list of advice for painting with acrylics. The list starts like this:

1.  Eliminate the white canvas as quickly as possible. Half of the painting is done as soon as the white disappears; this can be achieved in seconds by using a big brush.

2.  Set yourself a short time frame and stick to it. By allowing yourself weeks to finish a painting you will be unlikely to ever do so.

3.  Paint in layers. Rather than drawing shapes and colouring them in bit by bit. Start with the background, then paint on top of that, then paint on top of that, then paint on top of that. Thin washes of paint allow what is happening underneath them to show through.

4.  The drawing process happens throughout. By sticking religiously to your original sketch, you miss opportunities to improve and correct it as you go along.

5.  Keep looking. Spend more time looking at your source than at your canvas. Never say *screw it – I am just going to make the rest up.*

6.  Paint with the biggest brush possible, and slowly progress to smaller brushes. Starting with a small brush is like beginning to brush a horse with a toothbrush.

7.  Colour is everything. Clouds painted just in grey and white will look like they are made from concrete – look for their pale yellows, their delicate pinks, their twelve different shades of blue. Same goes for faces. Unexpected colours add

dimension, depth, life and character – no one is just one shade of peach.

8. Take photos as you go along. If you go make a mistake or go in the wrong direction, this will help you backtrack.

9. Step away. Walk to the other side of the room and look from a distance. Look at it in a mirror to see if it is balanced.

10. Do the final details after a good night's sleep. The decision of knowing when to stop is a big one. A good rest can help you make it wisely.

11. Do not use old mugs for your paintbrushes, or you will develop a bad habit of drinking paint water and dipping your brush in your cup of tea.

12. The world is your art gallery. Study the skin tones of people on buses. When you look at a cloud try to notice the softer edges and the sharper edges. When you go to the high street or buy a magazine look at how people are dressing and at how they are filling their homes. You cannot be a snob about your definition of art; art has been set loose on the streets – it is a free agent.

After leaving the bakery we walk around some of the local shops. Randy buys me a little tin sign that reads, "Only those who risk going too far will ever know how far they can go[30]." It is a T.S. Eliot quote. I hang it on a little hook in my mind. On parting, Randy asks me how much I would like to be paid for the art class. I say that their company is payment enough, but that if they feel uncomfortable not giving me money then I will accept it. Something is deposited in my hand as he shakes it in farewell – $500. I will be able to travel slightly more comfortably and buy more gifts to take home for my boys. A few weeks later I receive an email from Bee saying how thrilled they are to have added an English daughter to their collection of children. I am also thrilled to be able to add such a beautiful American couple to my collection of adopted parents.

On returning to Cat's house I find her angrily removing a satellite dish that a rental tenant has installed in her yard during her Scottish sojourn. The thick metal post with a substantial club foot of concrete is buried deep in the ground. She almost has it out already. When it is free, I offer to carry the heavy end. She looks at me with a look that only a woman in her fifties, who has raised three daughters, and lived alone in the highlands of Scotland could give. No. She will carry the heavy end.  I think that Cat is one of the first women I have met who I truly admire. Her strength is not a masculine strength; it is completely feminine. I find it remarkably beautiful. Sometimes, in order to grow and to change, we need someone to give us the permission to do so. We need someone to stand before us and to say: *This is who I am – being yourself is possible.* If someone does not provide us with that example, we can live our whole lives without ever knowing that it is. My time in Cat's house has been spent in the shadow of the sign that I remember from her previous house, *no stupid people.* It is like an invisible bar that I try to live up to, and not bang my head on. Strong women have standards, and I feel like I have been pulled up to them.

The next stop on my grand tour of America is the town of Bend: a beautiful mountainous area where the young people of Portland go to retire. I find out that one of Cat's four neighbours has a condo there, so I hitch a ride with him. It is a three-hour journey towards the interior of the state. The great grey expanses of fire-sacrificed Douglas fir stumps make a huge impression on me. I look at the countless scars on the landscape and acknowledge the forest's pain. I see how long such pain takes to heal.

Entering Bend, I am dropped off like a drug deal at a gas station where Bonnie picks me up in her big black SUV. I will tell you about Bonnie. Shortly before my trip began, she contacted me about a painting of a peacock she wanted to buy. Her problem with the purchase was that she did not have PayPal. I asked her where she lived, and when she said Oregon and described how beautiful Bend was, I said that I would be willing to deliver.

So here I am, painting in hand, ready to spend a few days with Bonnie and her family as they holiday in their RV on a campsite called *Sun River*. I like Bonnie instantly. As we drive, I start to put a face to my American customer base (I sell more paintings in America than I do in the UK). She is in her mid-fifties, with a deep heart and a great love for all things creative. I arrive at the campsite and put my bag up on the large bed above the cab of their RV. Looking around I slowly start to feel I have discovered The Real America.

The recreational vehicle that I am staying in with Bonnie and her husband is massive by British standards, but it is one of the smaller ones on the campsite. Some are bigger than my house, great Optimus Prime shaped trucks, referred to as semis. I get a tour of one. Owned by a silver haired man with the sort of paisley print shirt used by millionaires. His much younger, much slimmer wife is there too. All the surfaces inside are brass, and granite. There are inbuilt spotlights, flat screens, and tasselled curtains. The bedroom has a walk-in wardrobe. I ask how many guns he has onboard –

seven or eight, but he cannot show me them because they are not all legal in this state. I am starting to feel a little bit like the documentary maker Louis Theroux.

There is something wonderful about being suddenly immersed in a completely different culture. It is as invigorating as a cold shower and can be as life changing as a baptism. I was once asked if I would rather have good things happen to me, or interesting things – I said interesting. I am of course a seven on The Enneagram (if you have ever studied that), I am drawn towards adventure and new experiences. The thing is that the more that interesting things happen to you, the more interesting things you can handle. Curiosity has a snowball effect – it is a force which prevents increasing quantities of interesting things from ever becoming mundane.

One evening, I walk through the woodland campsite and meet a man who is excited to hear my English accent. He introduces me to his British wife, and we sit outside their camper (a responsibly sized converted pickup) and talk. They are a young liberal couple and a complete breath of fresh air. I run back to my RV and return with some packets of prawn cocktail crisps and chocolate left over from my night at BeerMongers. Chocolate is a good way to buy confidence. He is a police officer, and in eight years has only taken his gun out of its holster twice and has never fired it. He let me hold two of his handguns. I have a photo of myself, arms crossed in front of my body, gun in each hand. It is not a photo that I have shown many people. American gun laws are extremely strange to the British, myself included.

The campsite is bursting with chipmunks and ground squirrels. I suspect that maybe they entered into collaboration with the squir-

rels from Portland to come up with the next great coincidence: My
friend Shep from Washington State is visiting family in Bend. Bonnie drops me off outside their house. She has a brief visit to hospital
with a full-blown panic attack shortly after our teary farewell. Our
long talks bring a lot to the surface. Here is a poem that I write for
her after one of them.

### Broken

*You search for yourself in the mirror*
*You think you've lost her*
*You think you've lost her*
*To the shadows and the wrinkles*
*To the years of washing dishes and cooking meals*
*You think she's gone forever*
*So, you stay where you last saw her*
*You stay where you last saw her*
*You stay*
*Where you last saw her.*

*We walked, that night in Oregon*
*And remember how I told you*
*That though twenty years older*
*You are younger than I can ever be.*
*You are younger than I can ever be.*
*It's evening now and too dark to see*
*So, let me be your mirror baby*
*Face me and you will see*
*Nothing is beautiful until it's broken.*

*Face me and you will see*
*That*
*You're*
*Still*
*Here.*

She drives away, and I stare after her car until my sense of missing her is dislodged by the presence of Shep and his wife Mandy inviting me into the house. Shep is perhaps the coolest person I know. He was the best man at our wedding ten years previously, his relaxed aura enhanced by his sneakers and perpetually tousled hair as he stood in the church to play us a beautiful song on his guitar.

The house of his relatives (who are away during most of my visit at a conference for Jehovah's Witnesses) is large and comfortable, like a padded brown armchair that has moulded to the form of its chief occupier over the decades. We settle down for a cup of tea and a chat. The last time I saw him was nine years ago when we were both missionaries in Amsterdam. He had since settled in Australia with his young family; this is the first time that I meet his Australian wife. I ask Shep how he had been occupied during his time in Australia. When he does not answer straight away, I ask specifically about work. He looks at me like this is a strange question. "Well," he says, "I laid some carpets, I picked some fruit." I begin to realise that for Shep, work is not what defines him as a man. Shep just is. He does not need to his being to be referenced by such limited definitions. I ask him what his plans are for their big move back to the US. "I like growing things," he says slowly. "We might build a house on my parent's land in Washington State." He pauses again. "Life is for living not for working."

That afternoon we walk along the river and watch the paddle boarders try to make progress against its flow. We observe families being dropped off upstream to float down to the city on upmarket inner-tubes. An old man jogs past us as we watch slack-jawed. He looks at least ninety and is making some of the same movements that a jogger makes, whilst never going faster than walking pace. Such resilience in the face of obvious frailty is remarkable. The river draws people to its banks and carries them along in different ways. I match my stride with Shep's leisurely pace, following the focus of his gaze to the dappled reflections of water on the faces of his children.

I spend the night before I leave painting Shep and Mandy an Australian landscape to help bridge the gap between their two continents. Before being dropped off at the bus depot I look into Shep's bearded face and kind blue eyes and ask him what it is that keeps him clinging to his Christian faith. *Jesus*, he says, *Jesus*. Shep will always be a man of few words, but he means the ones he says.

Last time I hear from them, Shep is working as a window cleaner in Alaska. I am not surprised.

The bus takes me back towards Portland through winding tree-lined valleys. I stare through the window and spot a coyote in the middle of a field, face to the wind. The second our eyes meet I realise that he is rooted to the earth in a way that I can never be. I write this poem in the back of the book I am reading. The book is Sunset Song, by Lewis Grassic Gibbon[31], a story about the timelessness of the land and the spell that it casts on those connected to it.

## Poem for Oregon

*Oregon, I have met your dusty gaze*
*In the eyes of the coyote as he lies in the sun*
*Feet readied by memories*
*Of cowboys and men with guns*

*Oregon, I have seen your old men drive trucks*
*In caps that make them look like children*
*And run in string vests in the morning*
*As they have always done*
*Elbows angular as the peaks that watch them*
*Leaning slightly to one side*
*Charred like the Doug fir sentinels*
*Who remember forest fires*
*For decades.*

I sent a text to tell Quel that I would be arriving back in Portland at 2pm the next day. I wrote it late at night, and she reads it early the next morning. She says, "Great. See you tomorrow," promptly turning off her phone. I am usually a good communicator, but there are always plenty of lessons to learn. After a day wandering the city and a fascinating conversation with a man called Brian who left a job as an animator for the hit comedy show Portlandia to work in a coffee shop, I re-establish contact with Quel and move my things (all three of them) into the apartment that she shares with her new husband Tristan. I have a day or two before my flight to Kansas City – so – we take advantage of a window that appears between hospital visits and plan a brief honeymoon trip to Mount St Helens.

The unexpected diagnosis of leukaemia had put paid to their actual honeymoon plans. Portland is snuggled right up against the border with Washington State, and the volcano is only a few hours' drive up into it. I write a poem about the experience.

### Honeymoon on Mount St Helens

*The earth is a living thing*
*Breathing Boiling Erupting with rage*
*1980. As unexpected as a diagnosis of cancer*
*Two weeks before your wedding day.*
*"Life is weird" my friend tells me as she drives*
*Mount St Helens growing bigger on the horizon.*
*A topless mountain*
*Exposed and forever uncomfortable*
*Dormant now like his cancer had been.*
*We are in her shadow.*
*I take a photo of the newly weds*
*Washed in honey coloured light.*
*His head as bald as Helen's treeless slopes*
*Naked like the surface of the moon.*

We drive back slowly, the last tongues of sunlight licking the new green tips of the brave young fir trees who rise uncertainly amongst their fallen comrades. I finger a dried slither of wood in my pocket, a souvenir from one of the millions of trees felled like matchsticks by the pyroclastic flow that devastates two hundred and thirty square miles of forest in thirty seconds. It is like returning to a battleground forty years after the event and seeing all the bodies still lying where they have fallen – dry limbs pointing in the direction of their re-treat. The blast of hot volcanic gasses has removed even the top soil; we drive for what seems like forever before seeing signs of life seeping back into the forest.

When we get back to Portland, I pack my little yellow bag ready to fly to the Midwest. I am hoping to find some more real Ameri-cans, not these bicycle riding hippies so predominant to this upper left-hand corner. The next day I hop on a plane to Salt Lake City, hop off it, and hop on another one to Kansas City.

Marcia meets me at the airport. She has paid for my flight and in exchange I am going to give her as much artistic encouragement as I can. Kansas City straddles the states of Kansas and Missouri. Marcia lives in a small town on the Missouri side of the city, near the bank of the river of the same name. The drive from the airport doesn't take long, but it still allows us enough time to establish a friendship before I am invited into the house. It is a huge piece of wooden craftsmanship, built to blend in with its woodland setting halfway up a small hill. To crown the experience, the bedroom that I am shown into has a four-poster bed which is as wide as it is long. Both that night and for the two that follow – no matter how much I try to sprawl out and stretch my limbs – I don't think I once reach the other side.

The next morning, I am introduced to her husband Dan (a beautiful silver-haired biker) – he immediately realises how much he enjoys practicing what someone once evidently told him is an authentic British accent. "Ello," he says every time he sees me, drop-ping the "h" and shaking his head jauntily from side to side. I try

my best to not confound his expectations – echoing this pronuncia-
tion back to him with all the enthusiasm I can muster.

Marcia and I are so keen to get started in her little studio that
we don't have breakfast. We paint until well after lunchtime. When
we are done, I step onto her balcony to inhale some of the warm
September air and watch the squirrels doing their treetop acrobatic
routine. She follows me, and without thinking shuts the door behind
her. We are locked out – with only a small bag of almonds between
us for survival. This is somehow the exact moment when I realise
that food has become too much of an obstacle in my life. I am not
sure why – or how it relates to the squirrels and the almonds – but
since this point I have been able to control my intake of food. I can
lose the weight that I need to, without ever having to obsess over the
idea of dieting. Whenever I have a big life event, the squirrels are
always in the background, chewing on strings.

We call Dan to return from work early and let us back in. Marcia makes one of her signature salads with a tahini dressing and
thick slices of avocado. She is the sad evidence that, yet again, the
Americans I meet have a far healthier attitude to food than their
British counterparts. But the salad is good, and I am inspired rather
than disappointed by such a healthy attitude to food.

That afternoon we walk into town. I see groundhogs everywhere, which is weird because Marcia says that they are usually
pretty hard to spot – though of course it does occur to me that maybe I am seeing the same one over and over again. They quickly became my new favourite animal, and it would have been wonderful
for me to take one home for my sons. Fortunately, we stumble upon
a science education store called the H.M.S. Beagle and I am able to

settle on a more practical gift: a large jaw bone from the Missouri river. It is partially fossilised and most likely to have come from one of the bison roaming the area during the ice age. The human history in Europe may have been better documented, but America too has its own form of ancient history, drawn palpably into the present by the sheer scale and formidability of the landscape.

Marcia and I have a hoot painting together in the days which ensue. It is a relief to be indoors during the peak hours of Missouri's terrible September heat. I learn more from the people who I am supposedly trying to help than they do from me. Marcia's love of texture is contagious. She also introduces me to these wonderful things called interference paints. I have used them religiously ever since, and they add the most vibrant metallic sheen to all my paintings.

One of the highlights of my stay is a lady we meet on a trip to an art fair in Kansas City. Her name is Paula Winchester – in our opinion she is the sun around whom all other artists should circle. Paula stands surrounded by her paintings in a bright beret and glasses. Her curly grey hair frames the laughing face from which emanates a voice so high-pitched and expressive that she is the star of her own sit-com and we are the most avid of viewers.

Marcia spends $10 on a painting which is surely the pinnacle of all art created so far: a sketch of a sea-snail with a barnacle on its back and a tuft of seaweed growing off the barnacle. "Everything is connected!" Paula explains enthusiastically, "everything depends on everything else. Everything moves when we move. When I saw this snail, I knew that I just had to paint him. I love what I see, and I draw what I love. And you see what I see." I catch Marcia's gaze; we have just heard the loveliest possible summary of what it means to be an artist. The simple little painting reveals the soul of its creator. We can put down our paints; art has been done.

Kansas City is an amazing place to visit, the barbeques are all they say they will be, the fall pumpkins weigh more than I do. But like any true travel experience, it is the people who connect all these points on the canvas to create an image we want to remember. *Everything is connected. Everything depends on everything else.*

My journey back to Portland is a long one. My first flight is delayed by several hours, so it is a tired face that the customs officer looks into when a large jawbone appears on the x-ray machine. "I'm sure you're about to offer me a good and logical explanation for what I see here," he says. I offer it to him, and he reacts only with the slightest rolling of the eyes. He must have seen ten stranger things before breakfast.

I sit next to a fascinating gentleman and his dog on my flight from LA to Portland. I am not quite sure what the dog is doing here, but he says he has special privileges because his girlfriend is a flight attendant. I am happy because Joe is exactly the sort of person who I like to sit next to on long journeys – the sort of man who chops his own wood and forms his own opinions. His hat and sun-hardened skin makes him look wise and heroic. We talk about the dangers of capitalism, and the failures of the education system. We agree on everything; his logic seems bullet proof. This is until we start to talk about guns. Joe tells me that he lives in a cabin in the mountains to the east of Portland. I ask him if he has firearms. Four, he says: one under the sofa, one under his bed, one behind the front door and another in his bathroom cabinet. I ask him if he left them in a gun safe. "No," he says, "didn't even lock the door. There is no point, because there are no neighbours and it would be easy for anyone to break in if they wanted to." Gun logic – it seems – operates differently to other sorts of logic. We swap details, but I never hear from Joe again, nor (after hearing about the various signs warning that he will shoot first and ask questions later) do I feel overly tempted to visit his cabin unannounced. However, once in Portland, I do meet up with another hat wearing maverick who I met on a plane.

Rocky Blakewood calls to invite me out for dinner with his wife Deb. When they come to pick me up Quel comes outside to check who I am getting into a car with, but she is not overly concerned, after all, she has witnessed me climbing into the back of a van driven by five drunken nuns. Rocky and Deb are yet another beautiful example of American hospitality. We drive downtown and start our evening with a meal from the only place in Portland where anyone with any sense eats: a food van. Evenings like this leave me seriously confused. Is this how people here live? Do they leave their homes, spend time talking to like-minded people, eat food cooked by talented chefs and drink drinks served in bars with beautiful interior design and free live music? In my head the American life is other-worldly, remarkable even. Then, very slowly, it dawns on me that maybe some of these experiences can be found in the UK also. Maybe my amazement is mostly due to the fact that I have briefly escaped the domesticity of motherhood. Maybe I have not traversed the ocean and discovered an alternative universe. The truth of it does not matter really. The food still tastes better than anything I can remember tasting before, and the beer really is extremely good.

As full and as giddy as I am with my American adventure so far, it is not over yet – I am about to go to Idaho to meet Heidi.

She meets me at the airport, and I can see straight away that she is everything that I expect her to be after reading her emails. Heidi is magnificent. An attractive woman in her late thirties with a quizzical face like one of her pet parrots, and eyes perpetually wide enough to take in the whole world. She is a slightly nervous driver who manages to get lost once or twice when traversing the small city of Boise from the airport to her house. Heidi lost her father only a few weeks previously, and never attempts to hide the vulnerability this produces in her. She warns me prior to her visit that she might not be her usual self. I say this is OK, reinforcing my original statement that I am here to experience life as it is, not life with make-up on to disguise its flaws. Anyway – if this is the diminished version of herself – I can only assume that I would be overwhelmed by the undiminished version. She loves everything and everyone with abundant enthusiasm. She loves her little car, her little house, her little garden. When we go on a cycle ride down the river to take photos for the painting I am going to create for her, the beauty of the place where she lives is nearly too much and she almost collapses with sheer excitement.

While we paint Heidi tells me stories. My favourite is about the time she meets Alexander McCall Smith, author of the fabulous No.1 Ladies' Detective Agency[32], and The Sunday Philosophy Club[33] series featuring the character of Isabel Dalhousie. He visited the capital of Idaho a few years previously and Heidi seized the opportunity to connect with her favourite characters. She dressed up in a red dress like the one used by Isabel in the Scottish novels and donned a giant pair of African earrings such as might have been worn by Precious Ramotswe, the Rwandan detective. As soon as she had the chance to share a few words with the famous author she pressed a long letter into his hands, explaining passionately that it was addressed to Precious and to Isabel, that she had so much that she wanted to say to them, but that she feared her only chance of reaching them was through him. He gave her a bemused smiled and asked for her name. Heidi Juniper DeCoursey Clark, she said quickly. He beamed at her and said that he would have to put her in a book. In my opinion, Heidi should be in many books. It would not be too much if she were in all of them.

Heidi draws wonderful people to herself in much the same way as I seem to. One of her favourites is Grandpa Dave, a beautiful old gentleman in his nineties who comes to her for piano lessons. We pay him a visit one afternoon. The small flat is bursting with his art-work. One large painting shows a US Navy ship in Japanese waters. There is a small boat in the ship's shadow, in it a figure holding up a baby for the sailors to take. It was a scene from his past life that had haunted Grandpa Dave daily. Painting is cathartic he says. His art must indeed help him to keep his heart from becoming calloused, because Grandpa Dave's soul is like that of a child. I can see why Heidi loves him, and why she has made him part of her family.

I have somehow managed to collect an old licence plate from all the states I visited so far. It is nearing the end of my time in Idaho and I only have an hour in which to find one. I set out on foot from Heidi's house. I cannot help but photograph some of the houses. They are all so different and all so beautiful. Customised mail boxes and painted shutters. What I hate most about British houses is UPVC. White plastic windows, and white plastic doors. I feel like our houses have sold their souls in order to resist the damp. There is only one thing that disappoints me about America, and that is the lack of classic cars on the road. The cars they drive are new and black and shiny; it is not like the movies. I am pleased when I see a beautiful old blue ford rusting gently on someone's drive. A man comes out of the house and sees me staring at it. I ask him if it is OK for me to take a photo, and we chat as I do. I tell him that I am on a mission to find a licence plate, and he is kind enough to give me one.

The flight home is beautiful – even though I briefly get on the wrong plane and nearly end up in Arizona. The views through the window of the correct plane help calm my nerves after the episode. The desert mountains of Idaho sprinkled with the aspen trees that Heidi loves so much. Squares of farmland spread out like an endless tapestry, an ever-advancing monument to man's ability to dominate wild spaces. Then, suddenly, as if to refute our attempt to belittle nature – Oregon's majestic Mount Hood breaks like a giant through the clouds. Looking out to my right towards Washington State I can see the peak of Mount Rainier, another giant waiting on the horizon. Near her lays Mount St Helen's, broken to half her size, but still fuming. Evidence that the statements embodied by these mountains are not hollow.

I arrive back in Portland in the evening and take the MAX (a light-rail system that spans the city) back toward Quel and Tristan's house. I write a poem to capture the experience of the long walk home.

## Night Inhabitants

*Twenty-five blocks in the dark*
*I see no one but the moon*
*and the odd flash of a bus.*
*Portland hums to the silent frequency*
*of the street lamps,*
*her September air smells of sage and juniper*
*and of night owl coffee leaking through screen windows.*
*Something shifts my focus from the sidewalk,*
*a face presses up against a chain-link fence.*
*There is a gang of four on a vacant lot,*
*black and white,*
*bandit masks.*
*I watch without getting too close,*
*mesmerized by tiny hands*
*pulling seeds from pinecones.*

The racoons are terrifying. Mostly because of their cuteness
– and how it contrasts with their character. I am drawn to them,
pulling a torch from my handbag (or a flash light from my purse,
depending on your perspective) so I can get a better look. Most animals retreat if they don't want to be watched, but the racoons ad-
vance on me until I am the one forced to retreat. I am glad for the
presence of the fence.

It is now the end of September, and my birthday. Quel takes
me downtown to the iconic Voodoo Donuts to celebrate. Only in
Portland can you be served a bacon donut by a polite gentleman in
a Satanic T-shirt. The presence of bacon on everything is starting to

make me feel thoroughly American. I eat the donut whilst wearing a green visor cap, an ironic (though practical) purchase made at the campsite in Bend. If I was wearing white sneakers and long white socks, I would be fully integrated.

I spend the rest of my day with John and Karen (the beautiful couple who commissioned me to paint a portrait of their dog). The amazing thing about being an artist is that in spite of the fact that the customer has paid you for the painting that they have received, there is often still a surplus of gratitude. John and Karen take me out for dinner and introduce me to yet more wonderful beers from independent breweries. I try chili beer, then chocolate beer, later combining them to create a mole beer (based on the spicy chocolate so loved in Mexico). They gift me a pendant containing a tiny green jewel of a beetle. Karen and I share a deep love of bugs. My birthday card is made by John, a delicate drawing of a mushroom that I still have and treasure.

We are eating in the Pearl District, an old industrial area now famous for its stylish bars and gleaming lofts. There is a gallery called Hunt and Gather nearby and we wander in to look around. I am delighted to find art on the walls by Eli Halpin, an artist who I love and follow. Her bright oil paintings of comical animals dominate the space. I begin a conversation with the gallery owner about the possibility of my exhibiting there, she says that they only usually exhibit work by local artists. I tell her that I have been recently adopted by a couple from Eugene. Sometimes all you have to do is to hold on to your own logic as fiercely as other people do theirs. I have since filled one of their walls with a collection of my small paintings of bugs. My first suggestion was to provide them with a collection of birds on teacups – but they said that *putting birds on things* had been done to death in Portland.

The next day John and Karen take me to meet Mount Hood up close. We follow the Historic Columbia River Highway due East. Stopping only when the view becomes too spectacular for us to continue. Getting out of the car, I look down along the glittering span of the river as the warmth of the sun floods me from above. I breath in sharply and the moment lodges itself there. When my gaze draws itself back in, I become aware of a young man standing near me caught up in the magic of the same moment. He wears a T-shirt that shouts the words FUCK CANCER out into the beautiful void.

We stop again to take photos from the iconic bridge at Multnomah Falls. I always wonder about the weather system. Does that small section of water know it is part of a colossal recycling scheme as it plummets down for two hundred metres before hitting the rocks at the bottom? Will we only believe in rebirth if it actually happens to us? What is the life experience of a water molecule?

We continue driving. Mount Hood always right upon us, without ever seeming to get any bigger – like a mirage. Until suddenly He isn't there anymore and we are part of Him. We stop at the shore of a small lake – the moment as intimate as getting between a person and their reflection in a bathroom mirror. A little more altitude and we reach the Timberline Lodge, a massive structure and the only building for many miles around. The Lodge was built and furnished by local artisans during the Great Depression and was one of the locations in the movie The Shining. It is easy to understand how being surrounded by so much whiteness could leave space for mental imbalance. At such altitude, it seems that there is nothing to see but yourself.

I spend that night in John and Karen's beautiful home, a truly beautiful space furnished with large wooden pieces shipped back from the time they spent living in the Far East. A neighbour pops in to offer them a surplus rainbow trout, and I listen to them chat as I settle down at the kitchen table to paint a picture of Mount Hood for them to keep as a memento. Experiencing the inside of so many different American households is a fascinating thing. John keeps my wine glass topped up, and I paint until I am tired enough to fall asleep in the luxurious guest bed without reading more than a page or two of one the books left for visitors on the bedside table. It is a ghost story, but even coupled with thoughts of The Shining, it still is not enough to impede a beautiful night's sleep.

There is now only a day left before my flight. Quel takes me out for a drink and we look at each other over a giant mountain of nachos and cheese. I cannot decide if I feel like drinking coffee or beer – so I choose a coffee beer. Decision making in Portland is so simple. So much happened during my trip, without me having to try to force it. I don't once have to reach up to pick an apple from a tree, because they are falling all around me. When fruit falls it is usually because it is ready to eat. Not that the fruit always tastes great. I am, after all, sitting with a person who has just married someone with cancer. Quel has done the only thing that she could have, which is to follow the path that she is on. I would have done the same. I think we know – even as we take them – the decisions for which we will have no regrets.

At nine o'clock, on the evening before the morning of my flight, I meet up with my brother Andrew. He is travelling down the west coast with his girlfriend and happens to be in Portland at the same time as me. We spend half an hour together outside a Mexican food van, eating spicy tacos, and doing all the catching up that is possible in such a short space of time.

This final encounter seals the idea that I have squeezed as much as is humanly possible into my trip. Like I said at the start of my American adventure – life comes in waves. Sometimes these waves are insanely close together. Serendipity can be a drug that leaves you dizzy. It is good to plan recovery time between such highs. It is such a crazy dance, this life of ours, we cannot spend the whole time leaping and whirling. We must hold ourselves close too, and slow dance. Then we stand back, gazing with glazed eyes at the empty dance floor – wondering if it was all a dream.

Would it matter is it was? Dreams are a beautiful way to access the unconscious self. They give us crazy little metaphors to carry around in the pockets of our daily lives like worry stones. I do not want this particular dream to last any longer than it does; I want to get home to my kids.

CHAPTER 13

*Education*

It was not long after my trip that my husband left me. I hoped that the time apart would help the relationship, but instead it gave him the perspective he needed to be able to move on. He had wanted to go for a while, and I finally found the strength to let him. I was glad we had a ten-year anniversary party the year previously – a marriage of any length deserves a celebration.

I will never know how I would have dealt with divorce if I were the only person to worry about. Thank God I was not alone. I have had a deep connection with my children since before they were alive. I wrote them this letter when I was still a child myself. I kept it sealed in an envelope for decades and presented it to them when my eldest was nine—

To anyone who knows me as Mum,

As I am sure you can imagine this is a strange letter to write, so please bear with me. Writing to non-existent children is not an everyday task.

I do not yet know what it is like to be a parent, but like you I am also a child. I am hoping this letter will cause you to realise that we have more in common than you think. I intend to remember my views as a child when I am a parent. At the moment adults seem very boring. Above all

I do not want to become boring. If I ever do so, please remind me of this letter.

A funny thought –
I am in the present, you are in the future.
You are in the present, I am in the past.
–This letter is the only overlap

I wrote this letter to demonstrate just how easily the bridge of time can be crossed. I still feel inextricably linked to my childhood self, and I have not forgotten what it feels like to be that child – though I may have become more boring in some of the appropriate places. I am far from being a perfect parent: I am impatient, disorganised and often emotionally unavailable. Imperfection is something parents should talk about without shame. Sometimes I fail, but I try hard to be an example for my kids. Not just morally, but an example of the sort of life that I would like them to lead: a life full of joy and love for others. I don't want to just post words of wisdom on the bathroom mirror; I want to share experiences with them. I want them to believe in the power of serendipity and human connection. I want them to know that I see them as people of the present, not people of the future.

Recently – two years after my trip to North America – we had a vacation in Southern Spain. Sometimes my life contains excessive amounts of weird symmetry. I really love talking to old men; I think they are magical, like characters from story books – old Spanish men even more so. Two gentlemen are sitting on a bench in a village square and my boys and I introduce ourselves. They are lifelong friends, both called Miguel. Later that day there is another bench, presided over by two Pepés and a Juan. The trend follows throughout our visit with strings of men called Antonio and Carlos. Coincidence becomes a running theme.

One day stands out. We are in a small town of whitewashed houses nestled in the hills above the Mediterranean. There is a public pool that we can use for free, though it is a fifteen-minute walk from town and the midday sun is scorching. We are metres away, when Ty realises that he left his swimming noodle in the place where we ate. He declares loudly that it will be impossible for him to have any fun without it. This is devastating news. Rummaging around on the roadside I manage to pick up two plastic bottles. *Could I tie them together with my T-shirt to make a floating device?*

There is a man nearby, repairing a Volkswagen on his driveway. I make passing conversation about my experience with campervan conversion. He asks about the reason for our visit. I reply that I have given someone artwork in exchange for accommodation. The man with the van replies that he is also an artist. In less than a minute we are taken on a grand tour of his substantial property. He is a Gibralton called Graham, who has past involvements with YWAM and a house full of interesting people from a website called *Workaway*[34]. He is basically the male version of me, but with less hair and bigger muscles.

Boys are still desperately upset about the lack of swimming noodle and are wanting to leave. Eager to continue my conversation, I ask if they can use his pool – which is equipped with swimming floats of every description. My boys stand still for a while, stunned by the rapidity and random nature of the transaction. They are soon splashing in the pool, where they stay the whole day. I sit and chat and share food with Graham and his unusual household. The villa and the grounds are stunning. It is not his. There is a story about how the owner became a Christian in prison and decided that Graham would be its ideal caretaker. I might have some of the story wrong, there are so many stories that all overlap into each other. Graham tells another about a day when he really craves some fruit and prays that God will provide him with some. A Bulgarian turns up with a van full of fruit almost immediately, banging on the door and insisting that Graham takes as much as he wants.

Coincidences are interesting. The coincidence of meeting Graham is interesting – as if the universe folds in on itself a little to make it happen. *But why?* Just so my boys can have real swimming floats instead of something their mother strung together using a T-shirt and some water bottles? Quite possibly. I notice that the important thing about coincidences is not the size of the outcome. A big coincidence with a small outcome can be more beautiful than a small coincidence with a big outcome. When the mysteries of the universe confound us with their over exertion, they are at their most beautiful. God, if we are forced to use that word, often feels more tangible in the small things: benches lined with old men of the same name, the well-timed arrival of fruit, a perfectly located pool full of swimming floats. By focusing only on big life-changing events, we may miss the tiny golden molecules that even those big events are made up of. Children, it seems, are often closer to these truths because they have the ability to focus in on the tiny details that adults have trained themselves to ignore.

There is a quote from Ana Karenina that I have always loved.

*These joys were so trifling as to be as imperceptible*
*as grains of gold among the sand, and in moments*
*of depression she saw nothing but the sand; yet there*
*were brighter moments when she felt nothing but*
*joy, saw nothing but the gold. – Leo Tolstoy*[35]

I was still a child myself when I first read Ana Karenina. I remember hunting for a pen to underline these words and reading them over and over. I knew straight away that Tolstoy had given bodily form to what up until then had been little more than a ghostly concept in my mind. I was not so naively optimistic as to think that joy and beauty would be present in great quantities everywhere I looked. I knew that they were things that I would need to hunt for daily. I knew that objects in their vicinity would start to take on the same hue if I focused on them and contemplated them for long enough.

I don't spend every day of my life drawing my children's attention towards the magical golden threads that keep the universe spinning in infinity. I spend most of my time aggressively looking for odd socks and shouting at my boys for leaving the butter out for the dog to lick. I am more often a bad mother than a good one. Those who have children are often plagued with an unrelenting sense of guilt. Do I pick her up every time she cries? Do I let her sleep in bed with me? Do I worry if the only thing she eats is tomato soup? There are so many decisions to make, so much conflicting advice. Open-heartedness is the key to this. An open heart does not have to defend itself; it can make a U-turn in light of new evidence. I make – and continue to make – countless mistakes in my parenting.

My priority is to pursue what is right for them and for myself at any given moment in time. What was right yesterday might not be what is right today. Relating to children is not the same as relating to adults – because children are still growing. It is a relationship that cannot be fixed in its ways. I have two new people to get to know almost daily. It is a dynamic relationship and there is no danger of it becoming dull. Yes, many of the factors surrounding parenthood can become dull – but the children themselves can never be.

The same could be said of my relationship with Christianity. Anything that is growing and changing and throwing questions at you can never become dull. All these things are interlinked somehow – my questioning of religion leads to my challenging of the status quo in other areas of my life. When my children are unhappy after three years in school, I think outside of the box and consider all the options. Home education is a natural choice. It is my anger at the school that initiates the decision, but my love of home education soon takes over as the motivational force.

As a single mother, I needed to find a way to keep painting and to educate from home. Serendipity strikes again when a friend gives us a caravan. I do not need a caravan but say yes to it because I don't have a good reason to say no. A few days after parking it on the drive a mother who I meet in a home-ed group comes to visit. She tells me about the website *Workaway* (the same one used by Graham) which provides her with volunteers able to give an extra pair of hands when she needs them. I sign up straight away and house them in the caravan. It is this constant influx of foreign help which helps me to manage all the different projects that I have on the go.

Some people try to give their children the childhood that they didn't have. They want their children to be happy all of the time. They want to withhold the weight of responsibility from them for as long as possible. This often produces children who are overly reliant on their parents long term. I want to become obsolete. To raise children with survival skills. Children who can be self-motivated outside of institutions and rigid timetables. Above all – I want them to be engaged. Home education and *Workaway* has done this for them. Time out of the system – where they can be seen for the individuals they are – has allowed them space to discover the things they love about themselves and the world around them.

What open-heartedness and creativity require is the tearing down of boundaries. With religion it involves the removal of the line between the sacred and the secular, with education it is the scrapping of the idea that learning is something that takes place during certain hours. I home educated my boys for three years and have only recently re-entered them into the school system. This re-entering has not challenged my belief that education is an all-encompassing force that does not respect boundaries between school and home, classroom and the world in general. My willingness to send them back to school was for me an expression of my desire to always listen to my son's needs as they grow and change as people.

Here is a quick run through of some of the visitors who stayed with us during those three years: two young Spanish marine biologists, a passionately vegan dog trainer from Hungry and her German-Austrian boyfriend, a delightful German girl and her thirteen year old brother, a French YouTube star who absorbs the world around her like a sponge and reflects it back at itself with her videos, a nineteen-year-old Swiss skateboarder who can cook and mend things like a trained professional, an Australian with a passion for Japanese sword fighting with the twinkly-eyed patience of a saint, a deep-hearted singer and musician from Cyprus, a New Zealander with a love of Warhammer, a free spirited Paraguayan, a Jewish Brazilian with a love of musicals, a charming German of Afghani heritage, an American who manages to be both beautifully light-hearted and deeply grounded, an Indigenous Mexican hitchhiker who came to Europe with $10, an Irish American, her transgender wife and their teenage son, a young German girl with a passion for politics and poetry and her kind and helpful friend who accompanies her on a second visit, a young French law student with few words but lots of heart, a German philosopher who looks like a young Einstein. And last but never least, a beautiful Australian whirlwind of conflicting ideas and emotions who we adopt for her six-month stay and would have kept forever.

To all these beautiful adventurers:

We are so grateful to you for integrating into the homelife of the countries you travel through. For bringing us the world when we could not afford many foreign holidays. We are grateful for the many hours you spent on the trampoline, for the dog walking, for the endless card games and board games, for the den building, the cake making, the video editing. We are grateful that you gave us the chance to extend the boundary lines of our family. We include you in our love, in our childhood memories, in our dreams for a connected world.

My boys are now back in school. It is thanks to you that they are engaged with what they are learning. They see your face when your country is named in a geography lesson. They hear your accent in their language classes. They remember your encouragement when they want to give up. You nurtured the wild seeds of curiosity that are now growing up into strong, tall, beautiful plants.

Some say that *it takes a village to raise a child.*[36]
I say that *it takes a world.*

CHAPTER 14

*Community*

Not everyone is going to create community by hosting foreign visitors in their caravan. There are other ways too.

Have you ever looked at your neighbourhood and seen it as your home? As a space that belongs to you in the way that your house does? Have you bent down to pick up litter in the same way you would pick up something dropped on your own floor? Have you kept your voice down at night when you know you are near sleeping children, showing them the same kindness you would show your own?

Sometimes we feel so isolated in our little houses, but we are not – we are part of something much bigger. Tribal living has not disappeared, we have just lost sight of it. As long as there are other people on the planet, we can never be alone. If we feel bereaved, jilted, side-lined, or neglected then we are in good company because most people have felt these things too. People need people, and fortunately they are not in short supply. We need people to give us a lens through which we can know ourselves. We need people so we can swap skills and fit weaknesses with strengths like the edges of a jigsaw piece.

I heard of a man who joined a tribal community and was proud of himself for learning all the skills he could possibly need. The

Tribal Elders were disappointed because his self-sufficiency left no space for community to form. Asking a neighbour for a cup of sugar can be a way to start to draw a community together, especially if you give them a slice of the cake after you have made it.

*Joyce*

Acknowledging how geographical dispersal changed the role of family in my life, I decide to reach out to the local community to readdress the balance. With my own grandmother too far away for me to visit regularly, I feel a need to include the older generation in my life and the lives of my children. Simply knocking on someone's door and asking if they are lonely might not be the most helpful introduction, so I contact my local volunteer centre. They introduce me to Joyce, who has never married and has no close family. She is ninety-five when I meet her, and I visit weekly. Joyce has lived in the same house since it was built over fifty years ago. She refuses to update anything or to go into an old people's home. Visiting her home is like travelling back to the fifties, everything has been lovingly preserved just in case it might be useful. Joyce has been a school teacher and a staunch vegan for most of her life. She has a strong faith and strong opinions. I wrote down one of my last conversations with her—

*Joyce:*    My Aga provides me with hot water, I can cook with it.
It heats me kitchen and spreads around the house a bit.
I can dry me clothes with it. From the beginning they

said: *Get rid of your Aga and get a microwave.* Well that doesn't do all of those things does it?

*Emily*: You can't heat your house with a microwave.

*Joyce*: No no no no no. But it certainly gets difficult if you've got poor eyesight and it's getting worse. You've got poor hearing and it's getting worse. You've got a poor memory and it's getting worse. It's a forgettery. But I'm not giving in. But I couldn't eat me dinner.

*Emily*: You normally eat more than you did today.

*Joyce*: They've had a change around of my carers again. I tell the people in charge and they say they're glad to know, but the next rota they introduce is worse than the one before. Three of them came to visit me to tell me that they couldn't allow the carers more time for cooking vegan meals on the Aga. They tried to pressure me to get an electric steamer, and I said no no no. I'm not having it.

*Emily*: I'm sure that you'll outlive us all. You'll be here long after the microwaves and antibacterial cleaning products have killed us all off.

*Joyce*: I wasn't going to tell you, but perhaps I will. I'm not so steady on my legs as I used to be.

*Emily*: You've not had a fall?

*Joyce*: Yes. I fell here. I knocked the cassette player you bought me off. I don't think I've broken it. It was ages before I could get up.

*Emily*: Do you have one of those emergency alarms to wear around your neck?

*Joyce*: I had one. But the times when I'd use it are in the middle of the night when I can't breathe. And I wouldn't want to bother anyone. Twice I touched it by mistake and people had to come out. So, I won't use one.

*Emily*: But what would you do if something happens? If you fell and couldn't get up?

*Joyce*: I've fallen two or three times, and I've waited three or four hours. I will not wake anybody up.

*Emily*: But if you're on the floor! I'd come and help you. If you're in pain Joyce.

*Joyce*: I did hurt myself once, but the carer was coming in nearly five hours, so I just waited. The alarm system depends on volunteers and I couldn't find anyone for a long time. But they were elderly themselves. Young people are still working and they don't want to be disturbed. I'm so near the end I don't think it matters.

*Emily*: Could you not call an ambulance if you were in pain?

*Joyce*: It only happened once, and I managed. It proved to me that it's possible not to use the alarm system.

*Emily*: Don't feel that you're a burden to anyone Joyce.

*Joyce*: I'm happy the way things are. But I have to look after myself better. My leg just suddenly gave way and I was more worried about your cassette player.

*Emily*: You're a tough one aren't you Joyce.

*Joyce*:     Well it's not about me. It's about the young people now. It's their turn. I'll fall off the end soon to make space for them.

I am on holiday in Scotland when Joyce dies and I am devastated not to be able to attend the funeral. A few months after her death, I notice that her house is being cleared out for resale by one of the few remaining members of her family. There is a dumpster full of her possessions at the top of her drive. A truck has come to collect it, but I make them wait whilst I look for things to salvage.

## Joyce

*As she leaves*
*There is a tornado*
*Biblical*
*Twisting up into the sky*
*Like gnarled fingers*
*Junk mail from the 1950s*
*Sheet music from the 1890s*
*Broken Tupperware treasured*
*In case it is part*
*Of something bigger*
*Verses of advice*
*Scrawled on cereal box scraps*
*Twisting up into the sky*
*Like gnarled fingers*
*A whole fluttering cloud*
*Waiting up there now*
*Settling in*

*But refusing to get comfortable*
*Waiting for the right moment*
*To rain down*
*Words of wisdom*
*Words of humour*
*More than that*
*Surely words are more a person*
*Than a body is?*

*Five months ago*
*And fading*
*Like the ink on your childhood postcards*
*A forgettery*
*Of half invented words*
*Agrannoying*
*You would say*
*Complaining like an old lady*
*About microwave energy*
*And antibacterial everything*

*Here*
*Outside the silent tomb of your house*
*Watching birds in your garden sing*
*With no one to...*
*Here*
*like a stone rolled to the end of your drive*
*I find you*
*The whole of you*

*Ninety six percent of a century*
*Everything you ever*
*Wrote, touched, cherished, learnt,*
*Your whole life*
*In a box*

*And I save you*
*Tiny pieces of you*
*Flying petals of ash off your bonfire*
*I save them*

*The rest?*
*I watch as it is hauled away*
*The family watching me*
*Watching it*
*Family?*
*They wonder why I care about what is*
*Old and worthless*

*How I mourn*
*In these last moments*
*How I run around the metal box*
*Trying to reach your letters folded inside books*
*Trying to save your records from being smashed*
*Trying to wake you before they take you into the ground*

Even though she had no close family, Joyce still left a gap when she departed. She left a gap in my life; she left a gap in her community. I didn't enrich Joyce's life, she enriched mine. That is the biggest misunderstanding about community service; it is actually the community that serves us. There is a commonly held misconception among Christians that it is their role to be Christ to the needy, but Matthew 25 tells us that it is them who are Christ to us. Turning away someone in need is in fact turning away Christ himself. Could it be that in the moment of reaching out to fill the gaps in these people's lives, that we find that it is them who complete ours?

Meeting Joyce is one of the ways my neighbourhood has helped me fill the gap that would have been taken up by extended family, had modern transport links not enabled them to live further away. Neighbourhoods themselves are also threatened by our driving habits. We travel to visit friends who live further away, lessening the need for us to get to know our immediate neighbours. The fact that I don't drive is a huge aid in helping me nurture these relationships. I spent years getting to know all my neighbours. I talk to them about their problems and they listen to mine. I invite them round to play scrabble every week. I bake them cakes and they give me apples from their gardens. They walk my dog and I put their bins out. I make nearly a hundred pancakes for pancake day, and we spend every evening near Christmas in a different neighbour's house. They feel like family.

Slowly, I begin to realise that there is no formula for community. There is no one size fits all model. Community starts with an attitude. A state of mind. An ongoing openness of heart. Community reaches out to embrace all the people you meet. It is the act of non-judgement. It is the refusal to categorise or compartmentalise people. Charity work can be too structured and one-sided. Traditional neighbourliness can feel disingenuous. Filling your house with more people creates a closeness that does not always equate intimacy. Community is a spirit that cannot be boxed up and delivered next day – it is something that arrives of its own accord when the conditions are welcoming.

Slowly, I have begun to realise that the story of humanity as a whole cannot be told until the multitude of stories in the individual are listened to. You cannot talk about anthropological patterns, or about theories of human evolution, or about our inbuilt genetic need to operate communally - without first laying low and stalking these ideas at grass roots level, without listening to what they are saying when they whisper to each other. You cannot nurture community into existence until you know the people who compose it, and they know you. This willingness to know and be known is the definition of vulnerability.

Answers often come in the form of shared questions. We feel a sense of emptiness or a lack of fulfilment, and instead of looking to fill it we look for others who are also searching. Answers are false friends. Like the dream of the perfect partner who will sweep all your worries away, or the perfect daughter who will care for you into old age, or the perfect friend who will fill your life with joy. These people are often fictitious – but Joyce is real. She is what was. The twinkly-eyed old lady a few streets away. Bones like the boughs of an ancient tree laden with stories. An audible history book. A door that is always open and an empty chair waiting for a visitor. Fantasies are dangerous: we mourn the absence of relationships we do not have; we give up on people when we see their imperfections; we lose ourselves in dreams of what could or should be. We miss what is – because we are searching for something that is not.

CHAPTER 15

# Creativity

As with community – do we miss the art that is, because we are focusing on the art that is not?

Do we miss the creativity in our own life, because we are too busy admiring the creativity in someone else's? Please do not admire anything about me, for example. I am no less insecure than anyone else. So much of that admiration is pointless if it results in a dead end in your own creativity. This is one of the reasons why I enjoy giving art classes and helping people create art with their own name on it. That beautiful cross-over between community and creativity is what it is all about. Maybe we should look at other people's creativity as if it were are own – choose to see the whole creative world as one big collaborative picture.

It is a commonly held belief that some people are creative, and others are not. This – in my opinion – is bullshit. I meet and engage with different types of people from many walks of life and cultural backgrounds and have yet to find a truly uncreative soul. The art of painting alone contains something for everyone. It is a spectrum broad enough to shine light on every shade of ability. I have found that everyone approaches painting differently, but I have found no one unable to do it. I would go as far as to say that even unaccomplished artists have something to lay on the table that an accomplished artist could not offer, even if they wanted to. Naivety of line and the simple joy of basic self-expression are often watered down by the over-pursuit of perfection that comes with too many years of experience. Artistic offerings are as unique as the fingerprints of those who offer them, and though styles may differ hugely, their value does not.

We constantly need new ways to express ourselves creatively. It might be through sport, through cooking, running a business, writing. Even jobs and tasks not usually considered creative can easily become so if approached with an open heart and an open mind. A task like cleaning could be turned into a creative adventure. Questions could be asked to awaken creative processes: What is the fastest way to clean? What is the most fun way to clean? What is the most environmentally friendly way to clean? What is the most thorough way to clean? What is the most physically challenging way to clean? Before we know it, we could be saving time, the planet and our sanity by treating cleaning with the creative respect that it deserves.

What happens if we apply the same degree of creative thought to all the tasks we undertake? Lines drawn between what we consider to be a form of creative expression and what we see as something devoid of creative possibility become blurred. Our whole lives become one big creative experience. We inhabit the art we create. The best way to be an artist is to notice that you already are. You do not have to do anything more. You create whole worlds every time you open your mouth, your essence is expressed every time you move your face, and even when you sleep you surrender completely to your artistic identity – your dreams laughing and fighting and creating as energetically as children in a playground. This creative essence is so joyous that it opens its arms to all of the aspects of the journey. It enjoys the magic without trying to explain away the trick. It converts obstacles into opportunities.

I once painted trees on an old garden gate when I could not afford a canvas – and it was unique enough to make the front page of Reddit. I once accidentally splashed water on my canvas and when I wiped it off, some of the paint was removed too – a new effect was created that I have used ever since. I once made a beautiful mirror out of dozens of ugly old brushes because of an insane drive to recycle – and it became one of my favourite possessions. I was once given a broken canvas to repair and patched it with fabric – and was inspired to start adding fabric to more of my paintings. I once used a pallet that was too small, and all the colours touched each other – I now do this deliberately to encourage the accidental creation of unexpected secondaries and tertiaries. I once mixed fluorescent pink with standard pink because I had run out – I now often mix in fluorescents to add extra vibrancy. I once painted with the edge of a square brush when I could not find a small brush – I now believe that square brushes make a neater line. I once gave an art class to my Kiwi pilot friend Nathan because I thought it would be funny for him to fly home with a gorilla in the cockpit – and I realised for the first time that I was good at giving art classes. I once asked a friend to play his guitar while I painted because I could not listen to music and livestream because of copyright – and it has since become a regular occurrence. I once painted a picture instead of buying a birthday gift because I was a child and did not have any money – and I did that for all the birthdays, until eventually someone paid me and I felt brave enough to call myself an artist.

The biggest mistake I see people make when they paint it to stay unquestionably committed to the initial marks they make on the canvas. They miss countless opportunities to expand ideas because they do not listen to what the piece is trying to say. Re-draw. Re-see. Re-draw. Re-see. I don't even know which comes first. I don't even know if I am talking about art or life. Creativity is a living thing – it needs space to grow. It needs to be fed and watered. It needs to be cut back when it gets out of control. It needs seeds to be taken from it when it dies. If I could ask one thing of you it would be to nurture your creative life like it was a garden. Let it change with the seasons. Re-draw. Re-see. Plant new ideas. Create an artistic life that becomes a space you want to inhabit. A space that makes you feel alive. But most of all –

Enjoy it.

Self-expression has healing powers. A human's need for expression is primordial. Art gives voice to our inner world, and even if that voice is never heard, our inner self is still released into the otherness of the world outside us. We expand. We are released from the claustrophobia of our mind.

Creative types often suffer from depression. We take the whole world in with our wide hypervigilant eyes and the weight of it can sometimes be unbearable. Depression can be enhanced by the fact that we often feel a long way from the possibility of creative fulfilment, and a long way from the life that we would like to have. Melancholy sits at the other end of the same journey. Suddenly we have everything that we thought we wanted, and the knowledge that it still is not enough brings with it a whole new flavour of sadness.

The theologian Peter Rollins has taught me that depression and melancholy are both stagnant points at different ends of the same timeline. The only way to find lasting peace and occasional happiness is by finding a balance point somewhere between the two. We leave depression behind by believing in, and taking steps towards, an alternate future. We prevent melancholy by acknowledging that notions such as total stability, and permanent happiness are mere illusions. As soon as we decide that it is somehow possible to be satisfied with dissatisfaction, we can allow ourselves to live permanently in the sweet spot of the in-between.

Creativity is a tool which can help us navigate that space. It is a paddle which can direct us down rivers of the unknown, it is a smoke signal that can call people to our side when we get lost, it is a map that we can write to help fellow travellers who are following the same route. The best way for us to unleash the creative potential that will help us settle comfortably into this uncomfortable space is by understanding the concept of Flow. Flow has been defined as:

*"The mental state of operation in which a person performing an activity is fully immersed in a feeling of energized focus, full involvement, and enjoyment in the process of the activity.[37]"*

When flow is released into our lives there is no need for its influence to be limited to only one area. It has the power to help us live so completely in the moment that the whole notion of time can be momentarily transformed. We lose all sense of self, whilst paradoxically becoming more self-confident in the new knowledge of our true capabilities. The space that Flow takes us to can be so cocoon like that it can be profoundly healing. It has even been said that it is a space where people are less able to feel pain.

Flow is about much more than simply doing something which we find pleasurable. It requires both extreme challenge and the carefully honed skill set necessary to meet it. Mihaly Csikszentmihalyi is the architect of the notion of flow. He explains that it can be found somewhere in the space between anxiety and boredom. Anxiety often occurs when a person has the challenge without the skill set, and boredom can occur when they have the skill but lack the challenge that makes that skill useful. This fits into what I was just saying about Depression and Melancholy. We can be depressed because we feel overwhelmed by the challenges, and once our abilities have outgrown the size of the challenge we might be overcome with Melancholy.

We can avoid the pitfalls of Anxiety or Boredom, Depression or Melancholy by learning new skills that will instil us with new found self-confidence, and by taking on new challenges when the old ones have run dry. Take a moment to reflect: When have you experienced a sense of Flow? What skills do you have that you are not currently using? What challenges would help you use these skills? What current challenges do not have the skills for? What skills could you learn to help you meet these challenges?

Everything goes two ways. We cannot think of our art as something we should cling to with closed fists in order to keep our mental health intact in a world that seeks to destroy us. It is in the opening of our hands and the sharing of our art that we are able to reach out to others who are likewise struggling. It is only the second after we experience the deep loss of releasing our art into the world, that we realise that the act of giving is actually an act of receiving. Art can be selfish. Healthy creativity is open-hearted. There are narcissistic forms of art so intent on navel gazing and self-glorification that they release only negativity into the world. Art can be expressed in ways which deliberately exclude others, and in a world suffering the symptoms of isolation, this is an especially painful thing to behold.

All the topics I have covered in this book are interlinked. They are all different forms of the same journey: a letting go of the fear preventing us from being the person who we are, in the place where we are, with the skills we do or do not possess. What I am looking for really is a small crack in this fear. A way into the warm place that lays behind it. A way to help you open your heart in a sudden glorious blooming force of creativity. Creativity that has always been there, hiding in plain sight under all your actions. Open-hearted creativity that will envelop your relationships, and the way you engage with the world to find and bring healing. Creative freedom is a small catalyst that can lead to big change. Perhaps because it is one of the best and gentlest ways to summon the transformation brought about by renewed self-confidence.

Consider a few different creative artforms. If you feel that you have already found yours then great, but maybe there is something else out there waiting for you too – a whole new direction that you can head in, or a way you can expand or extend the art which you already know and love. I had already been painting my whole life when I decided to dedicate time to poetry and writing. It has been said that it takes round 10,000 hours to master something, that is 6-10 years. This can sometimes explain why we can get to a point in our life when we feel the sudden urge to start out on a new leg of creative adventure. It can be confusing to be in the place where we always wanted to be and to feel suddenly dissatisfied – like going on the same package holiday every year, before being overtaken with an uncontrollable need to visit a different country. If you ever succeed in getting close to the optimum levels obtainable from one artistic discipline, well then you can simply move onto the next – there are plenty to choose from. I started studying creative writing with the Open University at the age of thirty, which led to a love of poetry and spoken word. This filled a void that painting and draw-ing alone could not fill. It also linked back beautifully to my fine art. Hearing the sound of my own voice at spoken word events enabled me to embrace tools like livestreaming, and video creation. The more artforms we embrace, the more we can tie them together to create art that is increasingly complex, increasingly beautiful, and increasingly useful.

What it comes down to is creative hunger. The sort of hunger that is immensely satisfying, not in spite of its insatiability, but be-cause of it. That is the thing about art: there is always more. We can never truly inhabit that place of melancholy or boredom. We can never feel the complete dissatisfaction of having all that art can of-fer. We can never say that we have got to the place where we want to be, because perfection is unobtainable when it comes to art. George Harrison once saw a sunrise and said, "I want to do that.[38]" That is the insatiable nature of creative satisfaction. Harrison's desire to reach such heights was perhaps also representative of the depths of his artistic soul. The deeper you dig inside yourself the further beyond yourself you will want to reach.

My artistic journey is primarily about transcendence – about excavating the philosophical depths of myself in order to build a platform strong enough to launch from. I paint animals with halos and trees with roots reaching down like fingers to explore the earth. In Buenos Aires I painted giant wings on the wall of an abandoned warehouse, inviting people to stand in front of them, connecting for a second with their great transcendent self. Art for me is a reaching out in all directions. It is a general state of expansion and inclusion. It is the temporary illusion of wings painted on a crumbling inner-city wall.

Creativity at its best is about connection, collaboration, and about community. Maybe those things are about transcendence too? Creativity can work in opposition to the tide of disconnect and loneliness that washes up on the doorsteps of our carefully constructed houses. If we need our creative outlets to consume us completely, then there are three things to consider, a Venn Diagram of three overlapping circles: What do I love to do? How can I make money? What does the world around me need? There might be many things that give us a sense of flow. There might be many ways we can make money. The need around us might seem endless... Often there is only one small point where these three circles overlap. This point is a good place to start. Art can fit around our career and family life if we need it to – in small ways, in small doses, overlapping and underlying everything. Living artfully is like living prayerfully. It can be a state of being rather than an intermittent event.

I want to talk a little about my relationship with paint. We were not inseparable from birth. It was a shaky relationship growing up, and still is at times. My art teacher told me that any discipline that left curricular lines did not count. So, the relationship grew unhurriedly and privately behind closed doors in my bedroom as I tried, as teenagers do, to find an outlet for thoughts I did not have words for, and feelings I did not have thoughts for. It is only well applied time that can ever help us to get good at something – willingness to apply time like this only comes through obsession – we only become obsessed when we enjoy something – we only find enjoyment when not overwhelmed by frustration – frustration grows when we are unkind to ourselves. So, to be kind, I let myself cut corners and find shortcuts. I showed myself grace. I made up my own rules and turned art into a game I loved.

Growing older, my frustration with paint diminishes. We become comfortable in each other's presence; the sort of couple who do not need to talk to fill the silence. Age is teaching me that relationships go two ways, that I have to listen as well as make demands. I listen to the paint, to the quiet expectancy of the canvas, to the transcendent hum emanating from objects around me, to the voice beyond the voice I use in public. I listen to the vibrations between the eyes of my buyers and my creations. Only after listening, can I be presumptuous enough to give voice to the artwork, to let it say what it needs to. Art becomes conversation, a dance, a way to hitchhike through creative worlds, a prayer, a reaching for the unreachable, an embodiment of the invisible.

Relationships are the same thing: a reaching out for a state of oneness that can never be held for more than half a moment. A dance that we begin without knowing the steps. A journey that we start without a guaranteed destination. That sounds depressing maybe – but it's liberating. It removes the pressure of false expectations. Relationships cannot complete us – because we cannot be completed.

CHAPTER 16

# Relationships

So why do we try? Why do we try to complete ourselves with other people when we cannot be completed or to bottle a magic that cannot be preserved? Because that is the point, surely: art, religion, relationship – all limbs of the same tree reaching for the great transcendental other. It is such a beautiful process, like walking along a beach looking for shells that give hints of an underwater world. The oceanic oneness from whence we came and to where we will return when we die – if such a thing as death even exists. Expecting a permanent state of connection will only lead to disappointment. This understanding enhances the joy we can experience from moment to moment. It can help shatter the unhelpful illusion that other people's relationships are more complete than ours. When something is complete it is over. Relationship can never be over.

Are physical and emotional longing for romantic connection a form of prayer? Are all types of love in fact a form of worship? Not worship of the person we are thinking about, but of the unobtainable something beyond that. That makes it OK somehow. It makes the act of wanting and of loving an end in itself – whether the love is returned or not.

Love and relationships are two separate things. Love is not a magic spell that leaps out of the blue occasionally. Love is a constant. It does not pop out at an inopportune moment, like a fairy on a bungee rope, only to spring back to wherever it came from. Love is the eternal blanket that we are all wrapped in. The sea that we float in regardless of whether we choose to view the experience as sailing or drowning. Love does not come and go – it stays still – we are the ones who move.

The miracle of love is right in front of us – but we do not see it because we do not know what a miracle looks like. We look for love in one form and miss it when it appears in another. We look for lightening and rainbows, mountains breaking through clouds, for the perfect family home. We miss the sweetness of the grass growing up slowly and gently beneath our feet, the tired beauty of old paint flaking on a broken window frame, the old lady we walk past who chooses to give us her only smile of the day.

It would not be fair if love was only available to those in committed relationships. I think we all know, from what we have lived or what we have seen, that those in relationships call out in need of love just as much, if not more, than those who are single. Imagine feeling so loved that we do not need to have it affirmed by others. It is sadly not that straightforward. Learning to hold tight to the great thread of love which stitched together the fabric of the universe is not an easy thing to do. Deep down even the most seemingly confident people are plagued by a lack of self-acceptance. Sometimes all we need is a catalyst, a simple spark that will kickstart us on our journey. Someone who looks at us in a different way to how we see ourselves, someone who invites us to join them in that standpoint. Here is the good thing: when that person leaves our life, the love does not leave with them – because the love was there all along. We cling so tightly to people at times, terrified that they will one day see us for who we really are and then leave us. Or terrified that our own love for them will be revealed to be false. W.H. Auden describes it something like this:

> *When someone begins to lose the glamour they had for us on our first meeting them, we tell ourselves that we have been deceived, that our fantasy cast a halo over them which they are unworthy to bear – it is always possible, however, that the reverse is the case: that our disappointment is due to a failure of our own sensibility which lacks the strength to maintain itself at the acuteness at which it began. People may really be what we first thought them, and what we subsequently think of as the disappointing reality may be the person obscured by the staleness of our senses.*[39]

If we live knowing that the love given us cannot be taken away – we have power. Power to act as catalysts ourselves, to release an eternal wealth of love into the life of anyone who we meet.

If love is accessible to all of us all the time, why would we choose to go into a long-term relationship? I am not sure if that question is even answerable. I might respond differently to it depending on the day of the week. Today, I say that these relationships are a place where we can celebrate the love that we are already grounded in. A place where we can water and nurture that love so it can grow and reach out to all around us, giving them shelter and bearing fruit that can be harvested by passers-by. The seeds from that fruit grow into trees that expand the territory of our love. Love is indivisible. We cannot truly love our partner without loving the world around us and those in it. Love is a general outlook; if we hate one person it affects the love we have for others.

Romantic relationships show human connection at its closest. The parts of this uncomfortable proximity that we often see as the least helpful are often the most spirit enhancing. The childish reactions that make us feel like we are six again, the pain of being exposed when we would like to hide away from the world, the words that no one else would dare to say to us. We run away from friction because it feels uncomfortable, but if we allow it, this friction can weather away our hardest calluses and make our skin glow. There are of course times when conflict is not so easy to redeem. Sometimes we have a partner who uses moments of conflict for self-harm, rather than for self-improvement. In those times, we must protect them and ourselves by safeguarding their shadow, and by avoiding the traits of co-dependency. Therapy and counselling can help. There is always hope, even if the streets we are walking down are dark, we are never more than six feet away from stumbling down a deep well of hidden love.

Sometimes we do all the right things and it still is not enough. Despite the depth of our love, a relationship still ends, and we get hurt. It is ok to accept that there is nothing good about that pain, though it can still be valuable in its ability to bring growth. If manure can be used as a fertiliser, the pain expulsed from our past can be packed around our future to help it grow. Not all relationships last and that does not always mean they are less valuable or less successful.

I was married for eleven years, and I do not regret them. Love is still love wherever you choose to spend it. I am glad that I did not keep that love inside me until I met someone more appropriate. I am grateful that I have two beautiful boys as a result. I have even become grateful to him for leaving me, for this sweet gift of independence. I am grateful too for the deep pain I experience. My heart grows into it like a tree rooted into the precariously loose rocks on the side of a cliff. I learn to enjoy the views and to appreciate waking up every morning to find I am still here.

Singledom is a beautiful space for me. My bedroom is a place of refuge where I can read in the middle of the night with the light on and rustle pages to my heart's content. My house has become a joyous space where I alone am responsible for the atmosphere filling it. Kids from the neighbourhood trundle in and out without knocking. When my boys are asleep, I dance to music and wash the dishes in my underwear. I do not need other people to have a party, and I am certainly not looking to start another long-term relationship. My singledom is a beautiful gift and it will be extremely unlikely that I will meet someone for whom I will be willing to give it up.

Then I do.

I meet someone unexpectedly in circumstances dripping with unbelievable serendipity. I will call him Sam – but that is not his name. We look into each other's eyes and see reflections of ourselves. Every time he speaks, he answers one of my unasked questions. We are drawn to the divine in each other – like planets trying and failing to understand the forces of the universe.

I will not tell you the whole story; it is his story not mine. It is a very long story, with mountain peaks and valleys and winding rivers and open fields and deep dark woods. It is a story full of art and music and creativity and wonder and pain. So much pain.

After a year and a half, I wake up in his house and find that the story has ended. In the worst of all possible ways. I find that he has hanged himself, and I cut him down. I try to revive him, but he dies in hospital.

I realise that my grief is too wild a creature to conform to any stages. It does not follow; it leads. There is no order. It is the rabid dance of a lunatic, but a dance with steps, nonetheless. First step is basic survival. I delegate the care of myself to people from my church, trusting them to tell me which way is up, and which way is down. They put food in front of me and tell me what I need when I have no way of knowing. A small party of them visit my home, cleaning and reordering, so it will feel like a whole new space on my return. In the middle of the second sleepless night at my vicar's house I receive this email from Alaska. I've had no contact with Gabriel for twelve years.

Hi! It's been some time huh?

You often come up in conversation now that Shep lives in Alaska. Had some great times with you guys. I am writing you so randomly because I had a dream last night that I think means something. In the dream I walk into your flat or apartment or home. and instantly I know it has changed. It is as if I have been in your home before this time (in my dream I have memories of your home before this moment) so at this point I know that you have changed many things. I remember how your house had been full of color, and a bit chaotic, not dirty just quite eclectic. This time when I walk in everything is organized and all the walls are painted in soft blue. Before they were about 50 different colors and designs all over the walls. Now it is just one soft blue color everywhere.

I feel like God is doing this in your life, I believe He is wanting to and is bringing structure, clarity, order and most of all I think the blue has to do with peace. The difference in the atmosphere was drastic and beautiful. It was so calming and peaceful and restful. He wants to bring you into rest, where time slows down, and the littlest of whispers becomes the very thing that fills your heart and slows down the racing thoughts. I see you sitting in a cosy chair, sipping a cup of tea as the sun shines through the windows on your face and you have a gentle smile as your spirit and mind soak it all in.

I let out a deep sob as I read the message. There is a glow to it like I am reading a sacred text, a sense that God – if there is indeed such a mystery under that great blanket of a word – is going to fight for me as I fought for Sam. I feel some of the love that I gave coming back to me.

I call Gabriel and tell him my story. I hear him start to cry too. The cords of love reaching all the way from Alaska. He says that an old woman had approached him the night before the dream, to tell him that he is "God's Dream-Catcher." When we calculate the time difference, we realise that he had the dream around the time I found him.

My house feels different when I go home. The air clearer, like the blue air at the top of a mountain. I have a bath and use a bath bomb that Sam gave me for Christmas. It is red and foaming. After lying there for hours too long, I rise up out of it like a woman from a volcano –surprised I am still alive.

Then I turn to my art. Remembering how music had given Sam so much solace when his heart was hurting. I paint trees viewed from below. Fingers thinning and disappearing into the sky like a soul ascending. I paint in shades of blue, clinging to the peace of that colour with tired hands. Blue is an artist's representation of unreachable otherness: the great beyond, the mystical and the holy. I had painted Sam a kingfisher two days before he died. A small blue bird trying to be brave in the darkness of that night. It mirrored this poem I gave him not long after we met.

## Kingfisher

*I see a kingfisher this morning*
*Its blue bright against so much grey*
*And it reminds me of you*
*Of the way you keep singing*
*Through the darkest days of winter*
*The way you blaze a trail*
*between an empty nest and a broken branch*
*Your quiet song carried by the silence*
*Pushing the weight of the sky off your back*
*As your shadow skims the water*

*Other birds evade our sight*
*In the months when the sunlight*
*Is not there to bring out their colour*
*But your blue becomes more electric*
*And the fire in your chest*
*Does not need the sun to keep it burning*

*I wonder if Kingfishers give each other moral support*
*If they nod to each other across the water and say*
*Last night felt like it went on all day*
*But friend, just wait, these nights soon will be getting shorter*
*And the sun will demand that the world is filled with life again.*

And demand life it does. What else can I do but let my heart unfurl in the March sunlight? I love Sam through the winter, as I promise him with this poem not long after we meet. Spring never comes for us as a couple. But it will come for me, and it will come for him in a different way.

## Love in the Winter

*I love you with the sort of love that does not let go when it has had enough*
*I love you with the sort of love that changes according to the seasons*
*I love you with the sort of love that can lose its leaves and wait*
*Not bitter because it is not summer*
*But fitter and leaner*
*Exposed?*
*Yes*
*Cold?*
*Yes*
*But less buffeted by the winds and more able to see the view*

*I love you with the sort of love that has more than one outcome*
*I love you with the sort of love that has more than one season*
*I love you with the sort of love that has more than one reason*
*For wanting to reject the idea that love can be defined by a word*

*When it is the word that is defined by love*
*I love you with the sort of love that embraces*
*change in order to stay the same*
*I love you with the sort of love that loses leaves*
*so it can stand tall and watch you*
*Without being seen*

I still love him with love that changes according to the seasons. Seasons are funny things – not linear like we think time is – they run in circles and recycle themselves. Bringing me back to the very beginning, to the dream I have the night before I start to write this book. I talk to Sam until three in the morning, discussing whether our relationship is meant to be. I cry myself to sleep and fall straight into this dream:

*A broken butterfly fumbles its way around the kitchen floor. I have been observing it for a while, days, weeks maybe. Because of its beauty I long for it to live despite the impossibility of its situation. Someone comes through the door and I see it slip out past them. Cold and dark outside, my heart sinks, no chance for it. Then I see something strange; its damaged wings open and it begins to fly. Pinks and golds and yellows in the night sky. Oh, it is a moth not a butterfly – it is made for the darkness, it shines there. I do not squeal with joy – I almost cry with it. I see something else. A huge exotic green and gold moth. They are drawn together, as if by a light they each are making. Others appear, each of them also generating their own light.*

I think this means Sam and I are destined to be whole, destined to be together. Maybe he is simply destined to be drawn back into the healing heart of God's immense love. That his release into the sky that feels so very cold and dark does not mean the end of everything for me. Maybe the idea of destiny is not so linear. Maybe destiny folded in on itself somewhere and there is a distant corner of the Multiverse where he is alive, and we are together. Maybe destiny recalibrates itself like the seasons – a form of heavenly satellite navigation that recalculates a route every time we get lost.

I try to wait for my internal Sat-Nav to recalibrate. Nothing is clear. The only logical next step is for me to lose control of my senses. I write this poem.

### I should lose it now

*I should lose it now*
*I should run crying into the lake*
*And lay still and cold*
*Pale face surrounded by sad flowers*

*I should lose it now*
*Break all the plates in the kitchen*
*And stand screaming and motionless*
*Amongst shattered pieces of everything*

*I should lose it now*
*Burn all the clothes I wore when I was with you*
*Make a bonfire with all glances you gave*
*Flames flickering like mad eyes in the darkness*

*I should lose it now*
*Walk for days and leave my sanity in a forest*
*But I know it will just come back*
*Cold and bedraggled in the middle of the night*
*To stand shivering and resolute*
*Fists banging at my door*
*steady as a heartbeat*

There is no point losing something that does not want to be lost. I decide to do all the things I need to do not to lose it.

Around this time the philosopher and public speaker Peter Rollins invites me to a festival of radical theology in Belfast. Lacking a good reason to say no – I say yes. The name of the festival is *Wake* and the year's theme is *The Apocalypse.* The website gives an idea of what to expect:

> *Together we will unpack the dangers that arise as we confront an apocalypse in our personal, political or religious experience. More than this, we will carefully mine the potential that lies at the heart of such an earth-shattering event. As always, we will look at how pyrotheology can respond to the issues of our day; helping us live into the chaos of life. For apocalypse does not just mark the end of a world. It makes straight the paths for a new one.*[40]

It is a place to begin to address my raging torrent of internal questions ahead of the funeral, which is the day after the festival. A part of me wants to run from these questions – but they are too big for that – too scary –.and they move too fast. I know that I must be counter-intuitive and run towards them if I am going to survive, and I am a mother so non-survival is not an option.

There are about a hundred people attending, mostly American. Many, like me, have lived lives in the uncomfortable space between rational thought and religion. It is like finding new family members. A beautiful woman called Anna asks why I am there – I tell her a little of my story. She tells me that she has seen first-hand how female partners of suicide victims are often blamed, especially when they try to defend themselves. "Hold your head up in the funeral," she says, "surround yourself with light."

It feels like the whole event has been designed for me. There is a street art tour of the city. Showing where sectarian slogans have been replaced with images of hope. I think about how my creative collaboration with Sam had given me many opportunities to paint in public. I don't want to return to the isolation of my studio. I want to produce art that changes communities. I open my heart to the idea of cosmic recalibration.

One evening finds us in the upstairs room of The Sunflower watching Nick Cave's music documentary[41] about the death of his son. The pub was the location of shootings in the eighties. A security cage is still attached to the front door – now painted in a hopeful green and hung with flowers. Nick Cave speaks of eventually resorting to *happiness as an act of vengeance*. Can this violent space of grief be a place to plant flowers? Is that a possibility?

Everything is starting to come into sharp focus – I can hear more clearly, see things I never noticed, taste flavours I did not know existed. Weirdest of all is my propensity for laughter. We are told in one talk that life's beauty is in its ability to surprise and confound us, and that meaning can be found in the meaninglessness of life. Shortly after this (during the part of the program called *moment of wonder*) a man in a bra puts a monkey mask on a man from the audience, dubs him *monkey of truth* and makes him choose between puppies or kittens, and Catholics or Protestants.

Laughter acts like stabiliser wheels on the unstable bicycle of my pain and grief. No topic is too sacred or too dark. Maybe that is because laughter itself is a sacred thing. Laughter does not lessen my pain, it just holds it, gives it somewhere to rest for a moment. They need one another – comedy and tragedy, like two drunks leaning on each other as they try to guess which way is home.

The Friday after Wake I stand ten rows behind his coffin knowing that I have died with him. I carry the heaviness of more pain than I knew existed in the universe. I feel the full weight of Apocalypse. But I remember the words that were spoken to me in Ireland and I hold my head up and I surround myself with light. I call that light to myself – even though all I want is to join him deep in the earth. I remember how I feel when lying in the sun with my eyes closed, like something inside me is rising slowly like bread. Strange seeds disturbing the darkness of the earth. The Apocalypse blossoming.

We gate-crash a party in an expensive hotel late on the night of the funeral. My friend Toria and I say we are with the swing band and they play along, vouching for us when security tries to kick us out. We wear Venetian masks, hoping no one will notice that we are fifteen years older than the other guests. I have not danced like this before. Arms and legs moving in new directions as I navigate this new frontier between life and death. Music usually feels like a separate entity – tonight, it is part of me. I am one with the instruments, one with the room, one with the pain of the whole world – and the joy of it too. I am one with Toria, in the way that we always become one forever with those who are by our side at our greatest moment of darkness. But this whole thing is about so much more than darkness.

Sam is so much more than a passing storm. He is more than the pain of his parting. He is more than a traumatic event. He is more than a failed relationship. He is not a mistake. His death isn't my failure. If I could have all my hours with him again, I would do it all the same. He is a man worth loving, a man worth fighting for. I am glad I loved. Glad I fought. Not just for the chance to save him, but for allowing him to save me. I have heard people say that knowing or meeting him awoke something deep inside them, something that was sleeping so quietly that they had not known it was there. Thanks to him I am awake. I am alive in a new way.

So many things are alive now. So many stories have been born. Stories are metaphors. Sometimes they are more real than reality. My life with Sam is still real even though it only exists in that realm. I am writing alternative outcomes for myself and for him deep within my heart. They are truer to me than anything literal. The creative power of story is greater than the nostalgia for what could have been. The very same magic that could have spun the fabric of a future together – is the same magic that is forming the substance of the new stories unfolding in my life today. It is the magic I feel spin around me as I dance. Maybe the energy of the stories (that are written but not lived) gets reabsorbed into new stories. The stories are not dead in the same way that he is not. Everything is just enfolded into the great mystery of love.

In the beginning of this book I speak about how the church makes me try to force a conversion experience on myself. How I try to pin deep spiritual truths on a soul too young to hold them – repeating the equation of *crucifixion, resurrection and new life* over and over until the words lose meaning. Resurrection is a question. Big and echoing. Resoundingly hollow. A question existing without hope of an answer. The ghost of a question. A pale form that does not feel the need to haunt me because of my indifference to it.

That is until he dies. Then the question hits me in the face like a hook-shaped sledgehammer. It grows a body and walks behind me for weeks. I am not being haunted; I am being followed. My mind clinging to the image of the silver cross he always wore around his neck – like Dumbo holding the magic feather in hope that it will help him fly.

One day, two months after his death, my soul feels so heavy that I cannot move my body around the house to tidy up. I'm only good at tidying when people visit. No one is coming. I need a reason to tidy. I need visitors. Who could I invite? I want my house to be full of magic and miracles. Full of wonder, joy, healing and hope. So, I invite them. Why should they come? How will such things settle in a room that is dirty and cluttered? I tidy. I open doors to sunlight and birdsong and cold air. I stop fighting the darkness and open my heart to all of it.

The Buddhist monk Thich Nhat Hanh[42] talks of walking mindfully, embodying the words *I'm home home home* as each foot touches the ground. I wasted time arguing about where I was in relation to past and future. From now on, there will be no missed buses, no wrong places – just the now and the next step towards the next best thing. Coming down from this cloud of thoughts I notice there is a showing of the movie Mary Magdalene in my local theatre. It is the next step.

It is our movie. Our story. The pain in the face of Jesus every time he reaches out to heal someone is Sam's pain. The burden of a broken world is his burden. The pressure to be the man that everyone needs him to be, is his pressure. Mary's decision to accompany Jesus wherever the road leads, is my decision. Her decision to stare unblinking into the face of his pain is mine. Her dream of oceanic oneness, the watery narrative that underlines the movie, a friction-free place of pure connection, is my dream too.

The disciples think Jesus will usher in the dawn of a better world, maybe liberate them from the trauma of Roman occupation. Their pain is palpable and need for an alternative future critical. Sam is not just another brief relationship. He is the acumination of my hopes and dreams. He ties the loose ends of my life together. His presence in my life answers my unasked questions. I did not know someone like him could exist until I met him. The idea of a life without him is unfathomable.

Not many people know how Jesus' disciples feel to see him hanging on the cross. Witnessing the death of justice – the murder of unborn dreams. They have seen miracles, but so few of them. Not enough to make any real and lasting difference – a tiny ripple in an ocean of need. Together we have so many dreams still in an embryonic state. Our dreams could have transformed lives. It is a death of so many things, a death with so many layers of pain.

Just when I think that this pain is all there is, Mary's face cracks open like the clouds as he hangs there. The moment the real apocalypse of pain starts flooding in, the light floods in also. Like Sam's favourite Leonard Cohen quote, "there is a crack in everything, that's how the light gets in.[43]" My favourite line from the same song is, "every heart, every heart to love will come, but like a refugee." Broken. Tired. Restless. Increasingly aware that the journey is likely to continue getting harder. Knowing any shelter offered might be illusive – but also knowing that love can be carried along for the journey, that our homeland is within us whispering *I'm home home home* with every painful step. That love is an asylum from which we cannot be removed. A refuge that cannot be cut into pieces by borders and boundaries. That death cannot separate us from such love forever.

It is the darkest thing there is. Suicide. Crucifixion. Death. No one should have to go through it or to witness it. I want to turn back all of time to erase all of it, to save all of humanity from such immense pain – but I cannot – I can only do the next best thing. I can only look to the stories of hope that we cling to in order to plant seeds of hope in these darkest of places.

Mary catches the first glimpse of her resurrected Christ and thinks he is the gardener. Maybe he is. Maybe light refracts through Jesus onto humanity. Maybe resurrection is about multiplication not recurrence. The most moving part of that movie scene is seeing the face of Jesus washed clean of pain. Seeing the worry lines on his face look less like fissures and more like gentle paths leading out in a myriad of directions. I know that I would give my whole world to see Sam's face look like that. I know that maybe one day I will.

# Resurrection Songs

My response to Sam's death is to call for the multiplication of his open-hearted creative spirit.

*Everyone can sing,* he says often. *They just have to find their own voice.* Do we admire creatives, so we do not have to create? Is there a parallel between the worship of Christ and the worship of celebrity? Do we hang crucifixes and posters of popstars on our walls, elevating them to heights we know we will not reach? The humanity of Jesus is often underemphasised by Christians because worshiping someone is easier than following them. Someone dying on a cross to save us, saves us from the need to follow that example of sacrificial love. Radical love, and radical inclusion are things that we would rather avoid if we can. Great spiritual leaders and great artists should be followed rather than admired. We do this by viewing their creative spirit as an extension of our own. We multiply the deeply spiritual power of open-hearted creativity by adding our voice to the song. No single voice in valued more than another.

I call for this democratisation: Democratisation of creativity. Democratisation of spirituality. This is the call of the Open Heart: Equality. Radical inclusion. Outrageous love. These are the things I believe in. When death howls around them, these are things that stand tall and howl back.

It is this call that leads to the start of my next creative venture.

## Garbutt and Garcés

Not long after Sam's death my friend Toria asks me to join her on tour with the Punk Poet, Dr John Cooper Clarke, and (lacking a good reason to say no) I say yes.

I met and fell in love with Toria Garbutt in a toilet in Chesterfield. She had just read some of her poems at an event in the labour club and I think she is cool. Her poems are about drugs and boys – and other things that I do not know much about. I am surprised that she has time for me – but we find out that we both have sons of the same age, that we both home-educate, are both poets, both Librans, that we both just came out of 11-year relationships, and that we are both wearing black leather jackets and doc martens.

One night we are talking on the phone. *Night Garcés* she says. *Night Garbutt* I reply –and Garbutt and Garcés are born. It just sounds right. Like it needs a hashtag. Everyone knows that once something has a hashtag it instantly becomes a solid real actual thing. My ability to create coincidences and manufacture serendipity seems to be multiplied in Toria's presence. Rather than holding each other back we egg each other on, with often comedic results. Toria's poems are known for their dark and painful content, and I am in the most traumatic period of my life. Why comedy is surfacing at such a point is beyond us. I write this as one of many attempts to explain it to myself.

*Grief is as relentless as the sea. Sometimes massive waves crash over us and we feel like we are drowning. Occasionally, when*

*grief and joy collide like strangers on the street, a strange new*
*wave is created – and we can ride it to the shore and feel that*
*for half a moment we are flying. These moments do not decrease*
*the vastness of grief, but they do lesson its destructive power.*

This is one way to explain the inadvertent formation of our comedy duo, but there are others. Sometimes life gets so dark that the only way to call back the light is to laugh. Some truths are so unapproachable that the only way to draw near to them is under the guise of humour. The evil in our lives become so ridiculously dark, that the only response is to become ridiculous ourselves. In the words of my hero Frida Kahlo: *Nothing is worth more than laughter, it is strength to laugh and to abandon oneself, to be light. Tragedy is the most ridiculous thing.*[44]

Dr John Cooper Clarke is a performance poet from the North of England who shot to fame during the punk-rock era of the late 70s. Going on tour with him is a strange thing to do at the best of times; at the worst of times it is the only thing that makes sense. Toria opens for him. Standing straight backed on the stage. Feet a shoulder width apart. Arms moving in neat lines to mark out the sharp edges of her words. I sit in the audience, or backstage holding his gin and tonic when he takes the mic. The poetry pulses around me like the irregular beatings of my angry hurting heart. For a few days I lose myself in an ocean of words. I am held by them, buoyed up against my will. This is a space of solidarity. These are people who understand. Johnny Clarke's manager is Johnny Green, he also managed The Clash. Being with him is like watching a boxing coach getting his fighters safely in and out of the ring. He fights harder for them than they could ever fight for themselves. There are certain artists who have a right to that. A right to be fought for. A right to be held up and protected by everyone around them.

I take some beautiful mental snapshots during those few days. One of a tobacco salesman in our hotel bar, so happy for a chance to converse with John Cooper Clarke that he glows like the end of one of his cigars. One of Toria, myself, and poet Mike Garry on a balcony overlooking the sea after we are invited to the beautiful home of a family we meet at the merchandise stand. I take another of John Cooper Clarke's face as I act out all the details of some of my favourite toilet humour anecdotes in a posh hotel. I usually need to slow the pace of my delivery, but John's brain is wired to high frequency. Toria informs me that he is usually squeamish around such talk, but I seem to have go away with it. The barman says it is the most entertained he has been all week. When my anecdotes burn themselves out, I slump onto the couch next to him and offload all my problems. These celebrities have lived more lives than most, they have experienced more pain, gained more insight. "The universe is the backdrop to humanity," he tells me. It isn't what I want to hear. I want to hear that Sam's life doesn't matter. That he is one drop in an ocean of thousands. That I should let go. Forget. Move on. But I know The Doctor is right. All those stars are nothing compared with the beautiful universe I have seen spiralling inside the mind and soul of the man I love.

I spot a familiar face in the lobby of the hotel where we are having end of tour drinks – it is John Bishop, Liverpool's finest comedian. He is glancing surreptitiously over in our direction and I invite him over to join us. John Cooper Clarke has pushed down doors for others to follow in his wake, and today's stars seem to recognise him for the legend that he is. It is beautiful to witness the moments when these people meet.

Toria buys John a lychee infused cocktail and his nose wrinkles when he tries it. "What do you think?" I ask him. "I'm accepting it as an experience," he replies in his strong Liverpudlian accent. Toria is sitting with John Cooper Clarke on a sofa that faces the sofa where I am sitting with John Bishop. It is a surreal conversation that lasts into the small hours. I feel strangely at ease. After a while, John asks me why I am there. I tell him that I have had a very bad week, so my friend invited me. He asks for details and I advise him that the story might spoil his evening. He kindly insists, so I open up. I tell him my story, and he listens like it matters. Like I matter. I just lived through what feels like the most impossibly acute form of rejection, and yet here I am, being wined and dined in a beautiful hotel, surrounded by loving strangers. Important people. People who understand. People who are beginning to unpick the stiches of worthlessness that are lassoing my heart.

I vaguely remember John Bishop asking what I am drinking and me asking for a whisky, and him following suit and having a whisky also. It makes me feel good, like I am one of them. I vaguely remember giving John Bishop advice. Telling him to use his platform as a place to promote vulnerability. Telling him that we are all the same. Rich and poor. Ordinary and famous. That there are no boundaries separating any of our human nonsense.

This is not the hotel where Toria and I are staying (we are in Fawlty Towers down the road), but we decide to return for breakfast. We are dressed in yellow bandanas and I am wearing a pink charity shop jacket that makes me walk with fancy-dress confidence. The hotel staff have witnessed the company we were keeping the previous evening – they buzz around us offering drinks. The tour manager is apparently asked who the band is, and if we have something to do with Brian Ferry and Roxy Music. We think this is hilarious. We are all famous you see. Every last one of us. It is not about where you buy your jacket from – it is about how you walk when you wear it.

We sit down for a moment in the foyer and decide to livestream the moment in an episode called *Garbutt and Garcés read the papers*. We have just started when the concierge comes to check on us, unaware of the camera. I think he is still trying to figure out who we are. He tells us impressive stories about his encounters with celebrities as we ooh and ahh. His stories culminate with the confession that he was a butler for Michael Douglas on Bermuda for two years. *Oh wow. Michael Douglas*, we say in unison. When he leaves, I lean into the camera.

"Can't we be left to read our papers in peace. Madonna this Madonna that. Stevie Bloody Wonder. Who cares?"

"We were just trying to read an interesting feature on decorative eggs" quips Toria. "Which one is Michael Douglas, Garcés?"

Not many people are watching the video. But we think it is funny. The whole bloody thing is hilarious. We are in a hotel that is not ours, being treated like we are of great importance. We have proven many times since that it is not just because we are seen with famous people. If you believe that you are important – people treat you like you are. It is that simple. Self-belief is a form of self-love. Love that I am so in need of if I am to continue to be brave enough to stay open and love the world around me.

*Democratisation of celebrity. Democratisation of creativity.*
*Democratisation of spirituality. This is the call of the*
*Open Heart. Equality. Radical inclusion. Outrageous love.*
*These are the things I believe in. When death howls around*
*them, these are things that stand tall and howl back.*

I want to howl – to let that pain out of me – to give it a voice. Toria and I go to get matching tattoos. Anything will do. As long as it hurts. As long as it scars my body like my soul is scarred. As long as it releases some of my heart onto my sleeve. éte invincible. Invincible summer. From a phrase attributed to the French philosopher Albert Camus: *In the midst of winter, I found there was, within me, an invincible summer.* We plant it on our wrists like a seed. Like a decision to believe that the heavy darkness of the earth hides unseen promises of readying light. It lays waiting in the shade of my thumb. Believing that one day it will rise again, and that the journey will continue.

Seventeen years ago, I have a stupid idea to write a book about driftwood. I guess I have in a way. We are driftwood unaware that the tide is making us beautiful. Uprooted and transported in an unplanned journey by storms that we feel are destroying us. When the sun rises, and the sea is calm again – we feel buoyant enough to believe that it all makes sense. As those sunrises start to clock up, we learn to carry them within us, even during the storms. Internalising our *été invincible* amidst even the most terrible of winters. Those trees did not know they would become something else after they were felled. Like caterpillars waiting for death inside their cocoon, before bright beautiful broken wings open to spread their colour into the deep dark blue of the night sky.

Hitchhiking with Drunken Nuns is about the hope that embraces the messiness of the moment – it is about staying open to the surprises that arrive after missed buses. But it does not stop there. It goes as far as you are willing to travel. It accompanies you to death, and right through to the other side of it. Once we stop fearing the darkness, we feel ourselves being held aloft by it – spinning in impossible gravity like one of the stars. Someone recently asked me if I still believe in a personal God. I replied that my relationship with God is as personal as my relationship with gravity – it dictates every move I make; it holds me in place; it keeps everything turning so beautifully. Is the philosopher Paul Tillich's idea of God as the "Ground of Being[45]" less personal than a humanised God who rules from a cloud? What could be more personally attached to me than the ground I come from? What could hold me more closely than the air I breathe? Is this love the greatest and most personal of all the forces in the universe?

*Epilogue*

There is a storm called Gareth visiting the UK. No real aggression to him, just some clouds who want to share their bad mood with us. This morning my son forgets his school bus money and I run down the road in the rain with yesterday's yellow socks falling out the ends of my half-zipped trousers. I am winning at motherhood hands down.

My relationship with religion is going equally well – this afternoon I get into a confrontation with a street preacher. He is standing on the main shopping street in Sheffield with a microphone, shouting about hell and warning against homosexuality. The stall holders around him look weary under the dark weight of his words. I think the main reason I talk to him is to give them some reprise.

"Did Jesus turn anyone away?" I ask. Repeating the question until he is quiet enough to make eye contact. "Did Jesus ever turn anyone away? If Jesus holds the keys to heaven do you think he would shut anyone out?"

He tells me that Jesus warns more about hell than about anything else.

"Maybe you should listen to him," I say. "Maybe you should step away from all this darkness before it eats you alive. Maybe you should stop gnashing your teething and wailing. Maybe you should see the cross as his invitation to fight so hard for the weak and marginalised that the establishment wants you dead. You are going to annoy the authorities for exactly the opposite reason – what you are doing here is classed as hate speech. Love" – I say, gently trying to meet his gaze – "hell is the place without it".

A market trader raises his arms to me as I walk away.

"*Love!*" He exclaims. His eyes alive with it.

"*Love!*" I echo back at him.

The word resounds for a few seconds before the preacher lifts his microphone to continue.

I fight for these spaces. These seconds of clear quiet air amongst all the noise. It has been a year since Sam died, and some days are louder than others. This evening I sit at home slumped under the weight of it. I want my thoughts to put down their microphone for a minute.

"What's the meaning of life?" I mumble at Austin from my bean-bag (a young musician from Philadelphia who is visiting to help me with my garden).

"To breathe," he says, "and maybe to drink water".

I put the TV on and watch a movie called Hampstead. About a woman called Emily, also on the year's anniversary of her partner's death. The movie is about a shack hidden in the middle of a park where a reclusive man lives and grows vegetables. Sometimes the land wraps itself around us like that when we need a place to heal.

I think about the beginning of my story – my birth between the mountains and the sea. About how it felt to be rooted to the land and held aloft by the waves. I wonder about my escape to Argentina, and I start to think about missionary work in general. About phrases like *white saviour complex* – about how we run from our own problems and try to solve other people's. About how we talk about politics and judge how countries divide up their land and manage their resources. Maybe we should get our own house in order too, our own tiny square of land. My garden has been a mess for years; I do not see the point of lawns and am tired of feeling that gardening seems to mean fighting against nature. I don't want to fight it anymore – I want to surrender to life in the same way that some people surrender to death.

*I want to surrender to life*
*in the same way some people surrender to death*
*To lay back and let it take me*
*A four-poster bed, a river, a song in my head*
*I want to surrender to life*
*in the same way some people surrender to death*
*That person who knows how to make you angry*
*The enemy you live to fight*
*A garden weed, a bus ticket, a loosening thread*
*I want to surrender to life*
*in the same way some people surrender to death*
*To lie down, arms clinging to the ground, like it was my mother*
*A passing cloud, a shroud on the sunrise, that thing you said*
*I want to surrender to life*
*in the same way some people surrender to death*
*To give up alarm clocks, wake instead to the*
*smell of imagined coffee, a messy bed*
*A second-hand dream, an early flower, a first breath*

Austin is planting wildflowers for the bees and butterflies. I am going to dig a pond that will extend the habitat of the animals from the lake near my house. Maybe the kingfisher will visit. I want to learn to grow vegetables and to stop buying plastic. I want to learn to breathe and to drink water – to feel like a continuation of the weather system it has travelled through to reach me. I want to be part of the messy oneness of everything. I want to do more than live in the present moment – I want to live in the present place, with the present people. My house is rented, but I make it into a home regardless. I paint the walls colours that bring me peace. I do not want mindfulness to be an abstract word I cannot get hold of. I want to see it, to touch it, to smell it growing in my garden. All our homes are rented – the very nature of life is transitory. That is why it is all so beautiful.

*I want to surrender to life*
*in the same way some people surrender to death*

And I am learning to – slowly. For seven months after he dies, I listen to podcasts all the time – even as I sleep. I fill my head with positive content until the content starts to generate of its own accord. I do not sleep for many of these months. I see him as I had found him as soon as I close my eyes. Then I learn to repeat the words that are spoken by an angel to Mary Magdalene when she finds Jesus' tomb to be empty, over and over, like a mantra: *He is not here; he has risen, just as he said. He is not here; he has risen, just as he said. He is not here; he has risen, just as he said (John 20:11-18.)*

And I rise too – slowly. Not an external ascension – but an inward expansion. I climb into bed every night and climb straight into the place that some people can only access through psychedelics. I think – *Why not? If Heaven, or Oceanic Oneness, or The Kingdom of God, or Nirvana, or the Garden of Allah is a place – then why not go there?* The part of me that died with Sam, is there with him permanently, so it is nice to let myself feel almost in one piece occasionally. What funny creatures we humans are – so disjointed, so unaware – always caught up in this false dichotomy of reality and dreams.

*I am thinking again about the beginning of my story – my birth between the mountains and the sea. About how it felt to be rooted to the land and held aloft by the waves.*

It always makes me cry. I live right in the middle of the country and no matter how beautiful I make my garden, I will always be missing that part of me. Missing the ocean feels like separation anxiety – or like grief. I close my eyes.

Then it happens.

My mind is washed clean in a second. Salty baptism. Oceanic oneness. The invisible kingdom of God within me expanding and bursting like a water balloon. Tears stream down my face. All these years I think it is the ocean itself I am missing – but the whole thing has been a metaphor. A metaphor! And now – in my mind, or in something behind my mind – I have suddenly been given access to whatever it is that rages so beautifully behind the curtain of that metaphor. The ocean was within me all along. I can see it – hear it – smell it. But most of all – I can feel it. I have been on a long trip with some very drunken nuns, and –

I have come home.

# The Dynamic Feminine

## Tess Hall

It is time for change. I know you can feel it. There is so much to work on – climate change, social inequality, education – but is not a matter of working harder and faster. I think we are starting to realize that so much is not just far from completion – it is upside down. It is not just about putting society back the right way up. It is about finding a new way up. That is the power of the Dynamic Feminine.

I started following Emily on social media because it was clear to me that she was a true artist – not just with paints but in her thoughts and actions. I have never known anyone able to infuse so much creativity into something as mundane as cooking beetroots. I was only trying to absorb some of her artistic joie de vivre through online osmosis – but have instead found myself in a long-distance friendship that has led to me writing these words for her book. For anyone who knows Emily, this development comes as no surprise; she draws people to her, like moths to a light. She meets people with an open heart and open mind, and they meet her right back. She is a catalyst of connection, and the purist manifestation of the archetype of the Dynamic Feminine that I have ever known.

What is the Dynamic Feminine archetype? What is an archetype at all? These words may be new to you, but I promise that you do know them on an intrinsic level. This is because archetypes exist within you – are of you – and are exerting their influence in ways that are continuously felt even if they are not consciously understood.

Psychologist Joseph Jung[46] and mythologist Joseph Campbell[47] tell us that the human psyche consists of two dimensions: a conscious ego dimension (that which is our personal experience of subjective identity), and a collective unconscious dimension (an underlying awareness containing universal patterns and images that are shared by the whole of humanity). In more casual terms, the ego self is what one considers to be *me*: my body, my thoughts, my actions. It is a recognition of the individual self as we exist within the physical realm. The collective unconscious self goes deeper. It is a difficult concept to put into words, because it is beyond definition...but if one were to try, it could be called the oneness, the mystery, the source.

I like to use the metaphor of the aspen tree. You may have seen aspens before, dozens or even hundreds of them spilling across the hillside with their bright green leaves fluttering in the wind. Each one of these trees is connected to the others by an intertwined and interactive root system called a rhizome, and it is the rhizome that is the true organism. The trees are unique and lovely in their individual forms, but it is an illusion to see them as separate entities. So too with the ego and the Self. In this metaphor, the trees represent our individual ego forms while the rhizome represents the collective Self. Just as the trees need the endurance and stability of the root system in order to manifest physically, the ego needs the endurance and stability of the collective unconscious to manifest in the physical realm. Just as the trees bring the sweetness of sugar to the rhizome, our physical ego selves bring the sweetness of being known to the Self.

The shared universal patterns and images within the collective Self are called archetypes. They are not rational ideas or cognitive patterns, but rather forceful biological drives that require manifestation through the ego form. This is how the divine may see itself, through our human embodiment; *is the universe watching itself through my eyes?* Teenage Emily so eloquently asks. According to Campbell, these archetypes are shared by every single human being that has ever existed and can be seen in every culture around the world. They are the prototypical building blocks upon which individuals construct their perception of themselves and from which cultures construct their mythologies, and the path through which we may begin to know one another despite the differences of our personal experience and culture.

The dynamic feminine is one of these archetypes, and arguably the one that humanity has the most trouble with. This is why Emily's book and point of view are so meaningful – it is one thing to think and write about archetypes, and another thing entirely to live them.

In order to know the dynamic feminine divine, we must begin by observing the archetypal pattern in which it exists. Within each person's psyche, there are masculine and feminine principles exerting their influence. To be clear, your physical form and gender are not relevant, you have within you both masculine and feminine drives that need to be acknowledged and honoured.

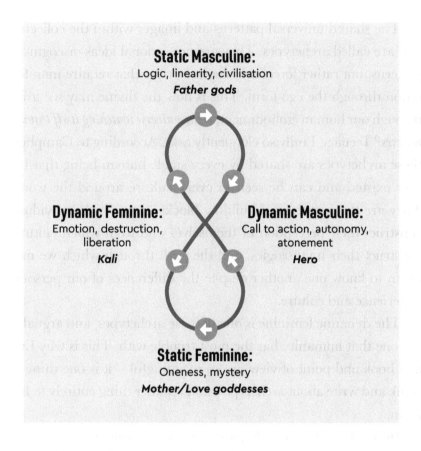

**Static Masculine:**
Logic, linearity, civilisation
*Father gods*

**Dynamic Feminine:**
Emotion, destruction,
liberation
*Kali*

**Dynamic Masculine:**
Call to action, autonomy,
atonement
*Hero*

**Static Feminine:**
Oneness, mystery
*Mother/Love goddesses*

The graph shows the four primary expressions of the masculine and feminine archetypes and how they relate to each other over a person's lifetime and collectively throughout society. It follows the cycle of Static Feminine ➲ Dynamic Masculine ➲ Static Masculine ➲ Dynamic Feminine ➲ Static Feminine and repeat.[48]

We begin in total connection with the oneness that is the collective unconscious of the Static Feminine. We are in complete and oblivious union with the source, the mystery, the watery ocean of the unknown. Mythologically, this the time for Mother goddesses that bestow unconditional caring and acceptance. The beginning of our separation from that oneness is the inspiration of creation mythologies across the world, from the Cosmic Turtle to the Garden of Eden.

So begins the Dynamic Masculine phase, which culminates in the story of archetypal Hero's journey. It is a story you know well – our world is infatuated with this tale, and it is told time and time again in literature and cinema: The Hero steps into the unknown and after much struggle and testing, succeeds and reaps the boon of his venture. While this boon is usually depicted as existing in the material realm (the princess is rescued, the enemy is destroyed) the true boon is meant to be the wisdom that was gained during the process of the journey and the ability to bring this wisdom back to share with the known world. In many stories the Hero discovers that the treasure had been sewn into the pocket of his cloak all along.

This initiates the Static Masculine phase: a time of structure and industry, creating and applying ethical and judicial codes, and the organizing religion. Linear thought and conformity are emphasized over emotion and self-reflection. Society organizes and strengthens, and people prosper. However, after a time many of the structures that were created during this phase may no longer serve the way it used too. People start to feel that the current methods of thought have become stale and inadequate. This creates division and unrest. People call for change. The systems that have held society in place begin to fall apart or are actively torn apart, without known new ones to take their place.

Thus begins the Dynamic Feminine phase, a time of great upheaval. The linearity and obedience of the prior phase are rejected, and subjective feelings and desires are elevated. Mythologically, this phase is one of the Trickster or Destroyer. Native American mythologies often depict this archetype through the mischievous Coyote who stirs up trouble, testing and violating moral precepts. His antics may seem maddening but are rewarded as often as they are thwarted. They highlight the parts of our lives that are nonsensical and frustrating, and gift us with laughter in the process. The goddess Kali is a darker depiction of this archetype. She is the Hindu goddess of death and destruction, often shown standing atop one of her victims, the head of another in one of her many dark blue hands, her tongue sticking out grotesquely. The image is meant to be terrifying – but she is often misunderstood. Kali symbolizes not a physical death, but rather a death of the ego as the illusion of reality. It is a liberation from the confines of the physical and external, and a call to reconnect to the oneness that is all. If properly embraced, we are then enveloped back into the static feminine, so that we may experience a watery rebirth and begin the cycle anew.

At least, this is how things are meant to unfold – instead, the current world exists in a state of over-identification with the masculine archetypes and repression of the feminine archetypes. Collectively – unconsciously – we are aware of the need for forward movement. Many of our current systems are not working for us and we want new answers. But we are too afraid of the psychic violence and pain that comes with this kind of dynamic change, of the rending of the very things that we have been told are good and right. So instead of taking the plunge into the dissolving Dynamic Feminine archetype, we are desperately grasping on to the phases of the masculine. Embracing the Dynamic Feminine will require balance – honouring both the archetypal Hero and its inverse, the Dynamic Feminine. An honouring not just of the firm structured Static Masculine, but also of the soft yielding Static Feminine.

That is why we need people like Emily. She writes that hers is *a journey of unknowing, culminating in a great unbecoming.* This is the wisdom of the Dynamic Feminine. The challenge is not the self-help culture fuelled change in who we are to become something more, but rather an unbecoming of the something else that has been thrust upon us by the social and cultural systems of our upbringing.

So how do we do this? How do we begin to embrace the feminine divine? By their very nature, the male archetypes are easier to consider because they focus on the external. The feminine archetypes are internal, subjective, amorphous. The possibility of containing them with words is the antithesis of the feminine divine – the moment you define it, you lose it. It is like a star that way; if you look directly at a star, it's light diminishes. It is best to look at it with your peripheral vision. It's the same with female archetypes. If we try to know the female divine using the same tools through which we have come to know the masculine archetypes, its brilliance will disappear.

Art and creativity are worthwhile places to start. They are a way for us to know the feminine divine without the confines of language. Campbell described artists as the *myth-makers.* The ones who create visual and poetic road maps for a society in transit. The Dynamic Feminine is a time for artists, both those that connect us to the beauty of the world and those who use their work as a platform for social change. Art defies containment. A blank canvas is infinite in its possibilities, as infinite as our ability for archetypal expression. It is an opportunity to transform not just a white square of cloth but also the artists themselves.

One of the most limiting things you can do as an artist is to prescribe at the onset what a painting is supposed to look like. Of course, one must begin with an idea and pursue bringing that idea into form, but if you dictate what you think should happen you are closing yourself off to the possibility of discovery. You are applying the constraining Static Masculine archetype to an activity better suited to the fluid perception of the Dynamic Feminine. As Emily writes, *mistakes can end up enhancing, rather than ruining the painting.* Engage in a conversation between you and the paint, between you and the idea. It is a symbiotic relationship between the artist and the art which it created. The author Elizabeth Gilbert believes that ideas are entities, floating around looking for someone to bring them to fruition. Taken this way, mistakes allow the entity/idea to guide you in a direction you may not have found on your own. Welcoming the new paths opened by error balances your ego self's need for unique expression – and simultaneously opens channels of expression for the great collective unconscious. If you allow yourself to be open to this, you may find that your work – and life – grow into something that expands beyond your perceived capabilities. This is what I think Emily means by *hitchhiking with drunken nuns* – A term which has come to symbolise the open embrace of anything which interrupts your travel plans: metaphorically, spiritually, creatively, and actually.

Art is transformative not only for the artist and the object they create, but also for the viewer. I think many people have had the experience of discovering a piece of art and feeling an instant – inexplicable – sense of wonder. You may be looking at a whimsical painting of an animal or at the stark marks of a continuous-line drawing – but in truth what you are looking at is a reflection of yourself. It is a feeling of being seen. *I love this*, you might say, *It's so me*. You cannot be seen without someone else there to do the seeing. The viewer and the artist become connected in the moment that this happens or, perhaps a better way of putting it, the art allows you to become aware of a connection that was already there. This is the feminine divine's drive toward oneness bubbling to the surface of our awareness. We are connected to so many others if only we make the effort to pay attention. Once we are paying full attention, all those dividing lines fall away; we look into the eyes of an old man called Ralph drunk on the concrete by a bus stop – and we see ourselves.

Emily's call for open-hearted creativity is a way to apply art to our everyday lives – even if we are uninclined to spend time with a paintbrush in hand – our very lives become the canvas. This can be done in any number of ways: Mindfulness is the art of bringing pur-poseful – non-judgmental – attention to the present moment and the tasks we are already performing. We can think of novel ways to experience activities we already enjoy. And we can start paying attention to the things that we have not yet tried but that are none-theless sending their feelers toward us. Emily decides to always say *yes* to a new experience, unless she has a good reason to say *no*. Have you ever looked at someone wearing a flashy outfit and thought, *I wish I could pull that off?* – you can. Have you ever watched someone on the dance floor and thought, *I wish I were a dancer?* – you are. These are moments when the divine is pushing against the confines that have been placed around her. She is begging you to leave behind your inhibitions and try something new – to become a fuller version of yourself. Listen to these moments.

Be curious. Pursue the unknown. Notice what scares you and then do it. Move towards – and through – the resistance. Wear something ridiculous. Try a new dish with an unpronounceable name. Ask the question you are not sure you should. Travel alone. Dance badly. Make mistakes. Paint something deliberately badly. Go wild swimming – or better yet: find your own manifestation of wild swimming – wild cooking? Wild singing? Really serious swimming? This book is not a template for what to do. It is Emily's story of how she was able to create metamorphosis in her life – the same things won't work for everyone. You have your own story, and you are the only one who can tell it. Our stories – our myths – are our great privilege as humans. We can elevate the moments of our everyday lives through conscious attention. It is such a fantastically huge responsibility. When you deny yourself the opportunity to radically become who you already are – you are denying the Divine the ability to know herself through you.

*Tess Hall is an artist, actress, and volunteer caregiver of children and cats.*

*She earned her BA in Humanities with focuses in Transpersonal Psychology and Fine Art from Sierra Nevada College. She lives in the idyllic foothills of Lake Tahoe.*

# Endnotes

1 F Zappa & P Occhiogrosso 'The Real Frank Zappa' Touchstone 1989

2 Joseph Campbell 'The Hero with a Thousand Faces' New World Library (2012 edition)

3 According to Shaine Claibourne, Munk wrote these words for a community newsletter shortly before being killed by the Gestapo in June 1944.

4 Dave Tomlinson 'Black Sheep & Prodigals: An Antidote to Black and White Religion' Hodder & Stoughton 2017

5 Richard Rohr 'Things Hidden: Scripture as Spirituality' Franciscan Media 2008

6 G Kendrick 'Shine Jesus Shine' Kingsway Music 1988

7 M Green 'There is a Redeemer' Birdwing Music 1982

8 R Founds 'Lord I lift your Name on High' Maranatha Music 1989

9 J Gibson 'Jesus we celebrate your victory" Kingsway Music 1987

10 I Smale 'Father God I wonder' Thankyou Music 1984

11 R Mullins 'Our God is an Awesome God' BMG Music 1988

12 R Mullins 'Hold me Jesus' BMG Music 1983

13 Nicky Cruz & Jamie Buckingham 'Run Baby Run' Hodder & Stoughton 2003

14 J Steinbeck 'The Grapes of Wrath' Penguin (2001 edition)

15 Anecdotal CS Lewis

16 N Page 'The Tabloid Bible' SPCK 2016

17 F Dostoyevsky 'The Brothers Karamazov' Penguin (1980 edition)

18 CS Lewis 'Little Book of Wisdom' Hampton 2018

19 CS Lewis 'God in the Dock' Eerdmans 1972

[20] F Dostoyevsky 'The Idiot' 1874 (Penguin 1980 edition)

[21] M Redman 'The Heart of Worship' Survivor Records 1998

[22] R Bradbury 'Farenheit 451' Ballentine Books 1953

[23] F Dostoyevsky ibid

[24] TS Eliot 'The Still Point of the Turning World' from 'Collected Poems' Faber & Faber 1942

[25] Leo Tolstoy 'Anna Karenina' 1873 (Penguin 1982 edition)

[26] Maya Angelou 'Still I Rise' Virago Press 1986

[27] www.theorderoftheblacksheep.com

[28] D Martin 'Volare' from 'This is Dean Martin' Capitol Records 1958

[29] Christoforo Armeno - English version of story of 'Peregrimaggio di tre giovani fi giluoli del re di Serendippo Venice 1537

[30] TS Eliot ibid

[31] Lewis Grassic Gibbon 'Sunset Song' Polygon 2006 edition

[32] Alexander McCall Smith 'The No.1 Ladies Detective Agency' series of books 1998-2007

[33] Alexander McCall Smith 'Sunday Philosophy Club' series of books 2004-2010

[34] www.workaway.info

[35] Leo Tolstoy ibid

[36] African proverb

[37] Colorado Association for the Gifted & Talented.. Original idea of flow attributed to Mihaly Cslkszemtmihalyi

[38] Anecdotal. Incident reported on Neflix documentary about George Harrison linked to Harrison's solo album "All Things Must Pass" 1970 Apple Records

[39] WH Auden '1929 Berlin Journal' quoted in Gerhart Meger & The Vision of Eros page 107

[40] peterrollins.com – to find out about Wake visit www.peterrollins.com/wake

41  "One More Time with Feeling" Iconoclast & JW Films 2016 Directed by Andrew Dominik

42  https://plumvillage.org/about/thich-nhat-hanh

43  Leonard Cohen 'Anthem' Colombia Records 1992

44  Frida Kahlo 'The Diary of Frida Kahlo: An Intimate Self-Portrait – Harry n Abrahams 1992

45  P Tillich 'Systematic Theology' Volumes 1-3 Chicago University Press 1951-1963

46  Joseph Jung 'Psychology of the Unconscious' Dover Publications 2003

47  Joseph Campbell ibid

48  Concept from G Hill 'Masculine and Feminine' London: Shambhala Productions